*"This could be Fr. Dulles' most significant theological work . . .*

"It is concerned mainly with ecclesiology. At the same time, however, it contains his thought on many other topics, such as revelation, ecumenism, eschatology . . . It is a thoroughly original work. Dulles touches on all of the significant literature in ecclesiology of the past 50 years, filling it, without forcing, into his scheme of the five models. Undoubtedly, this book ranks among the best that has ever been written in English on the subject."—*America*

". . . recommended both for those who wish to update their understanding of the Church and for those who wish to grow in their knowledge of the Christian community."
—*The Sign*

". . . an excellent study of a complex topic which is marked by Father Dulles' typical clarity of style and moderateness of tone . . . [The author's] combination of the catholic and the critical, in my view, represents Roman Catholicism at its best today."—*St. Anthony Messenger*

"*Models of the Church* will be a welcome addition to the survey literature in ecclesiology now available for seminary and college courses."—*National Catholic Reporter*

"It is not easy reading, but then the questions are not easy ones either. If it demands a little extra effort, the rewards are out of all proportion. It is, I should say, one of the most important contributions made to ecclesiology in our time."—*The Catholic Review*

"Those who have great difficulty getting excited by theological endeavors these days might suspend their disbelief and impatience for a while and look at Dulles' work. He is always a serious, sobersided kind of writer, and this book is no exception. But it is enlivened by a sense of what is happening in the world; he knows whereof he speaks in discussing these paradigms. Not for Catholics only."

—*The Christian Century*

"This book is the work of a professional. It has balance and breadth and a creative central theme. It will undoubtedly take its place beside such American classics as Niebuhr's *Christ and Culture*, Tillich's *Dynamics of Faith*, and James Gustafson's *Christ and the Moral Life* . . . It is full enough to be readily intelligible and suggestive enough to be eminently discussable."—*Theological Studies*

"I am pleased to commend *Models of the Church* as a monograph that gives us, in remarkably brief compass, an introduction to a vast literature and to a complex set of issues, and does so with fairness, clarity, and grace."

—*Commonweal*

"Dulles opens many fruitful lines of thought and shows how opposite poles of opinion both within the Catholic Church and among the Christian churches can be reconciled in a larger view . . . This [is] one of the most valuable theological books to appear in recent years of interest to scholars and general readers alike."—*Library Journal*

# MODELS OF THE CHURCH

# MODELS OF THE CHURCH

*Avery Dulles, S.J.*

*Complete and Unabridged*

IMAGE BOOKS
A Division of Doubleday & Company, Inc.
Garden City, New York
1978

Image Books edition by special arrangement with
Doubleday & Company, Inc.
Image Books edition published February 1978.

To
Gustave Weigel, S.J.
(1906–64)
teacher, colleague, friend
who taught me
to love the Church
and seek its unity

# Contents

# MODELS OF THE CHURCH

# Introduction

The discipline of comparative ecclesiology has for some years been practiced in ecumenical circles. The term usually signifies a systematic reflection on the points of similarity and difference in the ecclesiologies of different denominations. Attempting to account for the fundamental cleavages, ecumenical theologians have pointed to certain polarities, such as protestant vs. catholic, prophetic vs. priestly, vertical vs. horizontal, and institution vs. event. These categories, while illuminating up to a certain point, are in the end too dichotomous. To come flatly down on either side of these alternatives would be to content oneself with a half truth. The categories are too crude to express even the leading insights of any sophisticated ecclesiology.

This book attempts another variety of comparative ecclesiology. From the writings of a number of modern ecclesiologists, both Protestant and Catholic, I have sifted out five major approaches, types, or, as I prefer to call them, models. Each of these models is considered and evaluated in itself, and as a result of this critical assessment I draw the conclusion that a balanced theology of the Church must find a way of incorporating the major affirmations of each basic ecclesiological type. Each of the models calls attention to certain aspects of the Church that are less clearly brought out by the other models.

In selecting the term "models" rather than "aspects" or "dimensions," I wish to indicate my conviction that the Church, like other theological realities, is a mystery. Mysteries are realities of which we cannot speak directly. If we wish to talk about them at all we must draw on analogies afforded by our experience of the world. These analogies provide models. By attending to the analogies and utilizing them as models, we can indirectly grow in our understanding of the Church.

The peculiarity of models, as contrasted with aspects, is that we cannot integrate them into a single synthetic vision on the level of articulate, categorical thought. In order to do justice to the various aspects of the Church, as a complex reality, we must work simultaneously with different models. By a kind of mental juggling act, we have to keep several models in the air at once.

This book is written from a Roman Catholic point of view. In the popular mind, the Catholic Church is identified with what I describe as the institutional model of the Church. Catholics, therefore, are commonly thought to be committed to the thesis that the Church is most aptly conceived as a single, unified "perfect society." For reasons explained in this book, I hold that Catholics today should not wish to defend a primarily institutional view of the Church. Reacting somewhat against earlier concepts of Catholicism, I take a deliberately critical stance toward those ecclesiologies that are primarily or exclusively institutional. But throughout this book I insist that the institutional view is valid within limits. The Church of Christ does not exist in this world without an organization or structure that analogously resembles the organization of other human societies. Thus I include the institutional as one of the necessary elements of a balanced ecclesiology.

The most distinctive feature of Catholicism, in my opinion, is not its insistence on the institutional but rather its wholeness or balance (and here one might indulge in some playing on the etymology of the word "catholic" as the Greek equivalent for "universal"). I am of the opinion that the Catholic Church, in the name of its "catholicity," must at all costs avoid falling into a sectarian mentality. Being "catholic," this Church must be open to all God's truth, no matter who utters it. As St. Paul teaches, it must accept whatever things are true, honorable, just, pure, lovely, gracious, and excellent (cf. Phil. 4:8). Thus I find no conflict between being Catholic and being ecumenical. I hope I have succeeded in being both.

The basic idea of a typological approach to theological problems came to me some years ago when pondering the problem of faith and reason with the help of H. R. Niebuhr's classic, *Christ and Culture*. I found Niebuhr's five typical visions of the relationship between Christ and human culture exceptionally stimulating and helpful. Later, when preparing a paper on ecumenism, I was struck by the realization that the various points of view on the relationship between the Church and the churches are determined, to a great extent, by the models of the Church that one is presupposing. Ever since that idea arose in my mind I have had the desire to write a book expounding and comparing the prevalent models of the Church.

The number of models may be varied almost at will. In some presentations I have invoked as many as seven or eight. For simplicity's sake, I find it better to work with as few as possible, and for that reason I have here reduced the basic models to five. Each of these, however, could be broken down into several subtypes; and not every statement I make about the major types applies equally well to all the subtypes. This limitation in typological analysis has long been recognized as inevitable by sociologists, psychologists, and others.

It should be scarcely necessary to point out that no good ecclesiologist is exclusively committed to a single model of the Church. In drawing on various authors to illustrate one or another of my ecclesiological types, I am seeking examples of certain avenues of approach to the mystery of the Church; I am in no way seeking to pass judgment on the total achievement of the theologians I discuss. While picking out what is dominant in a given author's work at a certain stage of his career, or in a certain discussion, I am consciously leaving out things the same author may have said at another time and in another context. Thus, when I use Karl Barth to exemplify the kerygmatic approach to ecclesiology, I am quite aware that some of his later work could be used also to illustrate certain other approaches.

The method of models is applicable to the whole of theology, and not simply to ecclesiology. To a great extent, the five basic types discussed in these pages reflect distinctive mind-sets that become manifest in a given theologian's way of handling all the problems to which he addresses himself, including the doctrine of God, Christ, grace, sacraments, and the like. At various points in this work, especially in the chapter "The Church and Revelation," I touch briefly on the connection between the types used in ecclesiology and in the other treatises. I content myself with a few brief indications because my own categories in this work are deliberately selected with a view to ecclesiology. It is by no means clear that the appropriate categories for another treatise, such as Christology, would be the same. Other authors more thematically concerned with Christology—such as John McIntyre and James M. Gustafson—have come up with their own categories, which do not precisely correspond to mine or to each other's. It may well be that different models have to be forged to handle the material treated in different theological disciplines. To try to construct a basic typology valid for theology as a whole, and not simply for a particular branch, would be a much vaster enterprise than I have wished to undertake in this book.

The method of models or types, I believe, can have great value in helping people to get beyond the limitations of their own particular outlook, and to enter into fruitful conversation with others having a fundamentally different mentality. Such conversation is obviously essential if ecumenism is to get beyond its present impasses. Also, as Catholics have discovered since Vatican II, the problem of internal dialogue within a single denomination is almost equally acute. The Anglicans, with their principle of comprehensiveness, have come closer than most Roman Catholics to seeing the legitimacy of keeping irreducibly distinct theologies alive within the same ecclesiastical communion. To a certain extent, however, theological pluralism has always existed in the Catholic Church, as appears from the endemic tensions between the theological schools. The conflicts between Franciscans and Thomists, Augustinians and Jesuits are a matter of historical record. Since Vatican II, theological pluralism has been increasingly seen by Catholics as a desideratum. The method of typology pursued in this book should help to foster the kind of pluralism that heals and unifies, rather than a pluralism that divides and destroys.

Before concluding, I should like to express my sincere thanks to two friendly and exacting critics who have read this work in manuscript and given me some very helpful comments. They are the Reverend Francis A. Sullivan, S.J., of the Pontifical Gregorian University in Rome, and Dr. John S. Nelson of the Graduate Institute of Religious Education of Fordham University, New York City.

In several chapters I have used material that has appeared, in somewhat different form, elsewhere. Chapter IX, "The Church and the Churches," follows the main lines of my article, "The Church, the Churches, and the Catholic Church," which appeared in *Theological Studies* 33 (1972) 199–234. Chapter VII, "The Church and Eschatology," reproduces some of the ideas and expressions that are presented with fuller explanations and documentation in my article, "The Church as Eschatological Community" in Joseph Papin (ed.), *The Eschaton. A Community of Love* (Villanova, Pa.: Villanova University Press, 1973). I am grateful to the editors of both these publications for giving me permission to repeat some of the same material here.

*Avery Dulles, S.J.*

# I

# The Use of Models
# in Ecclesiology

In May 1972 the New York *Times* carried a typical exchange of views about what is happening in the Catholic Church in the United States. It reported the assessment of an Italian theologian, Battista Mondin, to the effect that the Church in America is falling apart. Two days later the *Times* published a letter to the editor in which the writer conceded, "[Mondin] is right that the traditional Church is near collapse," but then added: "The disasters he mentions are only such to those churchmen who are so stuck in conservatism and authority that they cannot see the Gospel of Christ for the Code of Canon Law. . . . My feeling, as a member of an adapting religious community, is that these are the best days of the church."

Disputes of this type are going on everywhere these days. Christians cannot agree about the measure of progress or decline because they have radically different visions of the Church. They are not agreed about what the Church really is.

When we ask what something is we are normally seeking a definition. The classical way to define a thing is to put it into a category of familiar objects and then to list the distinguishing characteristics that differentiate it from other members of the same category. Thus we say that a snail is a slow-moving gastropod mollusk, or that a chair is a piece of furniture designed for people to sit on. In definitions such as these we are dealing with external realities that we can see and touch, and we are able to pin them down fairly well in terms of familiar categories.

It used to be thought, at least by many, that the

Church and other realities of faith could be defined by a similar process. Thus the Church, according to Robert Bellarmine, is a specific type of human community (*coetus hominum*). "The one and true Church," he wrote in a celebrated passage, "is the community of men brought together by the profession of the same Christian faith and conjoined in the communion of the same sacraments, under the government of the legitimate pastors and especially the one vicar of Christ on earth, the Roman pontiff."[1] This definition, as contemporary commentators have noted,[2] comprises three elements: profession of the true faith, communion in the sacraments, and submission to the legitimate pastors. By applying these criteria, Bellarmine is able to exclude all persons who in his opinion do not belong to the true Church. The first criterion rules out pagans, Moslems, Jews, heretics, and apostates; the second rules out catechumens and excommunicated persons; the third rules out schismatics. Thus only Roman Catholics remain.

It is significant that Bellarmine's definition is entirely in terms of visible elements. He even goes so far as to maintain that, whereas *profession* of the true faith is essential, actual belief, being an internal and unverifiable factor, is not. A man who professes to believe but does not believe in his heart would be on this definition a member of the Church, whereas a man who believed without professing to believe would not be. Bellarmine's concern against the Reformers (especially Calvin) is to show that the true Church is a fully visible society—as visible, he says, as the Kingdom of France or the Republic of Venice. No doubt this concern reflects something of the spirit of the seventeenth century. The baroque mentality wanted the supernatural to be as manifest as possible, and the theology of the period tried to reduce everything to clear and distinct ideas.

This clarity, however, was bought at a price. It tended to lower the Church to the same plane as other human communities (since it was put in the same general category as they) and to neglect the most important thing about the Church: the presence in it of the God who calls the members to himself, sustains them by his grace, and works through them as they carry out the mission of the Church. There is something of a consensus today that the innermost reality of the Church—the most important constituent of its being—is the divine self-gift. The Church is a union or communion of men with one another through the grace of Christ. Although this communion manifests itself in sacramental and juridical structures, at the heart of the Church one finds mystery.

The term "mystery" has been used in many ways in the biblical and nonbiblical religions.[3] For present purposes, the usage of the Pauline epistles (1 Cor., Eph., and Col.) would be of central importance. The mystery par excellence is not so much God in his essential nature, or the counsels of the divine mind, but rather God's plan of salvation as it comes to concrete realization in the person of Christ Jesus. In Christ are "unsearchable riches" (Eph. 3:8); in him dwells the whole fullness of God (Col. 3:9); and this fullness is disclosed to those whose hearts are open to the Spirit which is from God (1 Cor. 2:12).

Vatican Council II, after rejecting an initial schema on the Church in which the first chapter was entitled "The Nature of the Church Militant," adopted as the title of its first chapter, "The Mystery of the Church," and this change of titles is symptomatic of the whole ecclesiology of the Council.

The term mystery, applied to the Church, signifies many things. It implies that the Church is not fully intelligible to the finite mind of man, and that the reason for this lack of intelligibility is not the poverty but the richness of the Church itself. Like other supernatural mysteries, the Church is known by a kind of connaturality (as Thomas Aquinas and the classical theologians called it).[4] We cannot fully objectify the Church because we are involved in it; we know it through a kind of intersubjectivity. Furthermore, the Church pertains to the mystery of Christ; Christ is carrying out in the Church his plan of redemption. He is dynamically at work in the Church through his Spirit.

When the New Testament tells us that marriage is "a great mystery in reference to Christ in the Church" (Eph. 5:32), it is implied that the union of the human with the divine, begun in Christ, goes on in the Church; otherwise marriage would not be a figure of the Church. In a word, the mystery is "Christ in you, your hope of glory" (Col. 1:2).

This general conception of mystery as applied to the Church was set forth by Paul VI in his opening address at the second session of the Council. He declared: "The Church is a mystery. It is a reality imbued with the hidden presence of God. It lies, therefore, within the very nature of the Church to be always open to new and ever greater exploration."[5]

The mysterious character of the Church has important implications for methodology. It rules out the possibility of proceeding from clear and univocal concepts, or from definitions in the usual sense of the word. The concepts abstracted from the realities we observe in the objective world about us are not applicable, at least directly, to the mystery of man's communion with God. Some would therefore conclude that ecclesiology must be apophatic; that we can have only a *theologia negativa* of the Church, affirming not what it is but only what it is not. In a certain sense this may be conceded. In some respects we shall in the end have to accept a reverent silence about the Church, or for that matter about any theological reality. But we should not fall into the negative phase prematurely, until we have exhausted the possibilities of the positive.

Among the positive tools that have been used to illuminate the mysteries of faith we must consider, in the first place, images. This consideration will lead us into some discussion of cognate realities, such as symbols, models, and paradigms—tools that have a long theological history, and are returning to their former prominence in the theology of our day.[6]

Referring to the debate on the schema *De Ecclesia* at the first session of Vatican II, Gustave Weigel, a council *peritus,* observed, in the last article published before his death:

> The most significant result of the debate was the profound realization that the Church has been described, in its two thousand years, not so much by verbal definitions as in the light of images. Most of the images are, of course, strictly biblical. The theological value of the images has been stoutly affirmed by the Council. The notion that you must begin with an Aristotelian definition was simply bypassed. In its place, a biblical analysis of the significance of the images was proposed.[7]

As Paul VI noted in the address already quoted, the Church has continually sought to further its self-understanding by meditation on the "revealing images" of Scripture: "the building raised up by Christ, the house of God, the temple and tabernacle of God, his people, his flock, his vine, his field, his city, the pillar of truth, and finally, the Bride of Christ, his Mystical Body."[8] These are approximately the same images used in the Vatican II Constitution on the Church, *Lumen gentium,* in its first chapter.

The Bible, when it seeks to illuminate the nature of the Church, speaks almost entirely through images, most of them, including many of those just mentioned, evidently metaphorical. Paul Minear, in his book, *Images of the Church in the New Testament,*[9] lists some ninety-six such images. Even if we rule out a few of these as not being really figures of the *Church,* we shall agree that the New Testament is extremely luxuriant in its ecclesiological imagery.

Ecclesiology down through the centuries has continued to meditate upon the biblical images. Following in the footsteps of Church Fathers such as Origen, the Venera-

ble Bede (eighth century) finds the Church in Eve and
Mary, in Abraham and Sarah, in Tamar, Rahab, Mary
Magdalene, in the woman with the flux of blood, in the
valiant woman of Proverbs, in Zacchaeus, the Canaanite
woman, the ark of Noah, the Temple, the vine, Paradise,
the moon, etc.[10] Thus there is nothing new in the fact
that images play a prominent role in contemporary ecclesiology.

In these images it is difficult to draw the line between
proper and metaphorical usage. For the most part, we are
dealing with metaphors, but we must reckon with the fact
that human language itself becomes bent by theological
usage so that figures that were originally metaphorical can
be properly though still analogously predicated. For example, terms such as "People of God" and "Body of Christ"
are often considered, in their ecclesiastical application,
something more than mere metaphors.

The psychology of images is exceedingly subtle and
complex. In the religious sphere, images function as
symbols.[11] That is to say, they speak to man existentially
and find an echo in the inarticulate depths of his psyche.
Such images communicate through their evocative power.
They convey a latent meaning that is apprehended in a
nonconceptual, even a subliminal, way. Symbols transform
the horizons of man's life, integrate his perception of reality, alter his scale of values, reorient his loyalties, attach-
ments, and aspirations in a manner far exceeding the
powers of abstract conceptual thought. Religious images,
as used in the Bible and Christian preaching, focus our experience in a new way. They have an aesthetic appeal, and
are apprehended not simply by the mind but by the imagination, the heart, or, more properly, the whole man.

Any large and continuing society that depends on the
loyalty and commitment of its members require symbolism
to hold it together.[12] In secular life, we are familiar with
the bald eagle, the black panther, the *fleur-de-lis*. These
images respectively arouse courage, militancy, and purity.
The biblical images of the Church as the flock of Christ,
the Bride, the Temple, or whatever, operate in a similar

manner. They suggest attitudes and courses of action; they intensify confidence and devotion. To some extent they are self-fulfilling; they make the Church become what they suggest the Church is.

Religious imagery is both functional and cognitive. In order to win acceptance, the images must resonate with the experience of the faithful. If they do so resonate, this is proof that there is some isomorphism between what the image depicts and the spiritual reality with which the faithful are in existential contact. Religious experience, then, provides a vital key for the evaluation and interpretation of symbols.

With regard to the Church Paul Minear has rightly said:

> Its self-understanding, its inner cohesion, its *esprit de corps,* derive from a dominant image of itself, even though that image remains inarticulately imbedded in subconscious strata. If an unauthentic image dominates its consciousness, there will first be subtle signs of malaise, followed by more overt tokens of communal deterioration. If an authentic image is recognized at the verbal level but denied in practice, there will also follow sure disintegration of the ligaments of corporate life.[13]

To be fully effective, images must be deeply rooted in the corporate experience of the faithful. In times of rapid cultural change, such as our own, a crisis of images is to be expected. Many traditional images lose their former hold on people, while the new images have not yet had time to gain their full power. The contemporary crisis of faith is, I believe, in very large part a crisis of images. City dwellers in a twentieth-century democracy feel ill at ease with many of the biblical images, since these are drawn from the life of a pastoral and patriarchal people of the ancient Near East. Many of us know very little from direct experience about lambs, wolves, sheep, vines, and grapes, or even about kings and patriarchs as they were in biblical times. There is need therefore to supplement these images with others that speak more directly to our contemporaries. The manufacturing of supplementary images goes on wherever the faith is vital. Today we experience some difficulty, however, since our experience of the world has become, in so many respects, secular and utilitarian. Our day-to-day life provides very few objects having numinous overtones that would make them obvious sources of new religious imagery—though there are some brilliant suggestions for new imagery in the writings of theologians such as Paul Tillich, Teilhard de Chardin, and Dietrich Bonhoeffer.

For an image to catch on in a religious community conditions have to be ripe psychologically. As Tillich used to say, images are not created or destroyed by deliberate human effort. They are born or they die. They acquire or lose power by a mysterious process that seems beyond man's control and even beyond his comprehension.

Images are immensely important for the life of the Church—for its preaching, its liturgy, and its general *esprit de corps*. We live by myth and symbol—by connotations as much as by denotations. In religious education a constant effort must be made to find images that faithfully communicate the Christian experience of God. Theology itself depends heavily on images. For theology, however, the unanalyzed image is of very limited value. The theologian is not primarily concerned, as the preacher is, with the question whether a given image is readily available and meaningful to the ordinary Christian in the pews. By using historical scholarship and empathetic imagination, the theologian can work with images that have lost their power and relevance for the majority of men today.

When the theologian uses images he does so for the purpose of gaining a better understanding of the mysteries of faith or, in the matter that interests us here, of the Church. He knows that images are useful up to a point, and that beyond that point they can become deceptive. Thus he employs images in a reflective, discriminative way. When he hears the Church called the flock of Christ, he is aware that certain things follow and others do not. It may follow, for instance, that the sheep (i.e., the faithful) hear the voice of their master (Christ), but it does not follow that the members of the Church grow wool. As a theoretician the theologian has to ask himself what are the critical principles leading to an accurate discrimination between the valid and invalid application of images.

When an image is employed reflectively and critically to deepen one's theoretical understanding of a reality it becomes what is today called a "model." Some models are also images—that is, those that can be readily imagined. Other models are of a more abstract nature, and are not precisely images. In the former class one might put temple, vine, and flock; in the latter, institution, society, community.

The term "model" has for some time been in use in the physical and social sciences. I. T. Ramsey, among others, has shown its fruitfulness for theology. When a physicist is investigating something that lies beyond his direct experience, he ordinarily uses as a crutch some more familiar object sufficiently similar to provide him with reference points. Billiard balls, for example, may serve as models for probing the phenomena of light. Some models, such as those used in architecture, are scale reproductions of the reality under consideration, but others, more schematic in nature, are not intended to be replicas. They are realities having a sufficient functional correspondence with the object under study so that they provide conceptual tools and vocabulary; they hold together facts that would otherwise seem unrelated, and they suggest consequences that may subsequently be verified by experiment. As I. T. Ramsey has said, "In any scientific understanding a model is better the more prolific it is in generating deductions which are then open to experimental verification and falsification."[14]

As Ramsey's analysis shows, the term "model," as employed in modern physics, is practically synonymous with analogy, if this latter term is shorn of some of the meta-physical implications it has in neo-Scholastic theology.

Having seen a little of the use of models in the physical sciences, let us reflect on the transfer of the method of models to theology. Ewert Cousins has written lucidly of the similarities and differences between the two fields:

> Theology is concerned with the ultimate level of religious mystery, which is even less accessible than the mystery of the physical universe. Hence our religious language and symbols should be looked upon as models because, even more than the concepts of science, they only approximate the object they are reflecting. . . .
>
> To use the concept of model in theology, then, breaks the illusion that we are actually encompassing the infinite within our finite structures of language. It prevents concepts and symbols from becoming idols and opens theology to variety and development just as the model method has done for science. Yet there is a danger that it will not go far enough, for it may not take sufficiently into account the level of religious experience. The theologian may copy the sciences too closely. He may take the scientific method as a normative model. . . . In so doing the theologian may not take into account the subjective element at the core of religion. The religious experience has a depth that has no correlate in our experience of the physical universe. The religious experience touches the innermost part of the person. . . .[15]

Taking these remarks into consideration, one may perhaps divide the uses of models in theology into two types, the one explanatory, the other exploratory.

On the explanatory level, models serve to synthesize what we already know or at least are inclined to believe. A model is accepted if it accounts for a large number of biblical and traditional data and accords with what history and experience tell us about the Christian life. The gospel parables of growth, such as those of the wheat and the tares, the mustard seed, and the leaven, have been valued because they give intelligibility to phenomena encountered in the Christian community since its origins, for example, its capacity for rapid expansion, the opposition it encounters from within and without, the presence of evil even in the midst of the community of grace, and so forth. These images suggest how it is possible for the Church to change its shape and size without losing its individuality. They point to a mysterious life principle within the Church and thus harmonize with the biblical and traditional doctrine of the indwelling of the Holy Spirit. These botanical models, however, have obvious limits, since they evidently fail to account for the distinctively interpersonal and historical phenomena characteristic of the Church as a human community that perdures through the generations. Thus societal models, such as that of God's People on pilgrimage, are used to supplement the organic metaphors.

The more applications a given model has, the more it suggests a real isomorphism between the Church and the reality being used as the analogue. The analogy will never be perfect because the Church, as a mystery of grace, has properties not paralleled by anything knowable outside of faith.

By the exploratory, or heuristic, use of models, I mean their capacity to lead to new theological insights. This role is harder to identify, because theology is not an experimental science in the same way that physics, for example, is. Theology has an abiding objective norm in the past— that is, in the revelation that was given once and for all in Jesus Christ. There can be no "other gospel" (cf. Gal. 1:8). In some fashion every discovery is ultimately validated in terms of what was already given in Scripture and tradition. But even the past would not be revelation to us unless God were still alive and giving himself to mankind in Jesus Christ. Thus the present experience of grace enters intrinsically into the method of theology. Thanks to the ongoing experience of the Christian community, theology can discover aspects of the gospel of which Christians were not previously conscious.

For example, we shall be considering in a later chapter the Servant model of the Church. This is a relatively new model, based on the biblical image of Israel, and later of Christ, as Servant of God. The recent application of this model to the Church has made us conscious in our time, as our forbears were not conscious, of the Church's responsibility to assist the welfare of man on earth and hence to contribute to social and cultural life.

With respect to the heuristic function of images, there is a particular problem of verification in theology. Because the Church is mystery, there can be no question of deductive or crudely empirical tests. Deduction is ruled out because we have no clear abstract concepts of the Church that could furnish terms for a syllogism. Empirical tests are inadequate because visible results and statistics will never by themselves tell us whether a given decision was right or wrong.

In my own view, theological verification depends upon a kind of corporate discernment of spirits. John Powell, S.J., shows that this type of spiritual perception is closely connected with the "connaturality" to which we have already referred. Thanks to the interior presence of the Holy Spirit, the whole Church and its members have a new life in Christ.

> As this life of Christ is deepened in us by the Holy Spirit, there is created in the Christian a "sense of Christ," a taste and instinctual judgment for the things of God, a deeper perception of God's truth, an increased understanding of God's dispositions and love toward us. This is what Christians must strive to attain individually and corporately; theologians call it Christian *connaturality*. It is like a natural instinct or intuition, but it is not natural, since it results from the supernatural realities of the Divine Indwell-

ing and the impulses of grace. No account of
dialectical or analytical facility, which is purely
human, can provide this connatural instinct. It
is increased only by the continual nourishment
of the life of God that vivifies the Christian.[16]

Thanks to this grace-given dynamism toward the things
of God, the faithful, insofar as they are docile to the
Spirit, tend to accept whatever in their religious experience leads to an intensification of faith, hope, and charity,
or to an increase of what Paul in the fifth chapter of
Galatians calls the fruits of the Holy Spirit—love, joy,
peace, patience, kindness, and the like (cf. Gal. 5:22–25).
Where the result is inner turbulence, anger, discord, dis-
gust, distraction, and the like, the Church can judge that
the Spirit of Christ is not at work. We assess models and
theories, therefore, by living out the consequences to
which they point.

Paul VI points this out in his first encyclical, *Ecclesiam
suam*: "The mystery of the Church is not a mere object
of theological knowledge; it is something to be lived,
something that the faithful soul can have a kind of connatural experience of, even before arriving at a clear notion
of it."[17] In our present context one might say: Because the
mystery of the Church is at work in the hearts of committed Christians, as something in which they vitally participate, they can assess the adequacy and limits of various
models by consulting their own experience. A recognition
of the inner and supernatural dimension of theological
epistemology is one of the major breakthroughs of our
time. In this type of knowledge, theory and practice are
inseparably united. The Church exists only as a dynamic
reality achieving itself in history, and only through some
kind of sharing in the Church's life can one understand at
all sufficiently what the Church is. A person lacking this
inner familiarity given by faith could not be a competent
judge of the value of the models.

An example might clarify the method of discernment I
have in mind. In the Middle Ages, the notion of vicarious

satisfaction took on great importance in the theology of penance. With the increased acceptance of juridical models of the Church in that period, there resulted an elaborate theology of indulgences. The theory was applied to practice, giving rise to a vigorous spiritual traffic. Financially the theory succeeded: The empty coffers of the Holy See were replenished. But was this success a confirmation of the theory? Only the evangelically sensitive Christian could judge whether the effects on the spiritual lives of Christians were those intended by Christ for his Church. Martin Luther carried many of the faithful with him in his protest, which was, at least in part, based on deep evangelical concerns. Since the sixteenth century the Church, I think, has come to recognize that there was much justice in Luther's complaints regarding indulgences. This recognition calls for a theological response that has not yet been fully worked out in Roman Catholic theology. A model that leads to practical abuses is, even from a theoretical standpoint, a bad model.

As already stated, the models used in theology are not scale reproductions. They are what Max Black calls "analogue models" or what Ian Ramsey calls "disclosure models." Because their correspondence with the mystery of the Church is only partial and functional, models are necessarily inadequate. They illumine certain phenomena but not others. Each of them exhibits what can be seen by comparison with some particular reality given in our human experience of the world—e.g., the relationship of a vine to its branches, of a head to a body, or of a bride to a husband. Pursued alone, any single model will lead to distortions. It will misplace the accent, and thus entail consequences that are not valid. For example, the analogy of the head and body would suggest that the members of the Church have no personal freedom and autonomy in relationship to Christ and his Spirit. In order to offset the defects of individual models, the theologian, like the physicist, employs a combination of irreducibly distinct models. Phenomena not intelligible in terms of one model may be readily explicable when another model is used.

Admitting the inevitability of such a pluralism of models, theology usually seeks to reduce this pluralism to a minimum. The human mind, in its quest for explanations, necessarily seeks unity. A unified field theory in theology would be able to account for all the data of Scripture and tradition, and all the experience of the faithful by reference to some one model. At various times in the history of the Church it has seemed possible to construct a total theology, or at least a total ecclesiology, on the basis of a single model. Such a dominant model is, in the terminology of this book, a paradigm. A model rises to the status of a paradigm when it has proved successful in solving a great variety of problems and is expected to be an appropriate tool for unraveling anomalies as yet unsolved. I am here employing the term "paradigm" in approximately the meaning given to it by Thomas S. Kuhn. He speaks of paradigms as "concrete puzzle-solutions which, employed as models or examples, can replace explicit rules as a basis for the solution of the remaining puzzles of normal science."[18]

As a model succeeds in dealing with a number of different problems, it becomes an object of confidence, sometimes to such an extent that theologians almost cease to question its appropriateness for almost any problem that may arise. In the Scholasticism of the Counter Reformation period, the Church was so exclusively presented on the analogy of the secular state that this model became, for practical purposes, the only one in Roman Catholic theological currency. Even today, many middle-aged Catholics are acutely uncomfortable with any other paradigm of the Church than the _societas perfecta._ But actually this societal model has been displaced from the center of Catholic theology since about 1940.

In 1943 Pius XII gave quasicanonical status to the image of the Mystical Body. "If we would define and describe this true Church of Jesus Christ—which is the One, Holy, Catholic, Apostolic, Roman Church—we shall find no expression more noble, more sublime, or more divine than the phrase which calls it 'the Mystical Body of

Jesus Christ.'"[19] The Mystical Body analogy reached its highest peak of popularity between 1940 and 1950. In the late forties theologians became conscious of certain deficiencies in the model and attempted to meet these by appealing to other models, such as People of God and Sacrament of Christ.

Vatican Council II in its Constitution on the Church made ample use of the models of the Body of Christ and the Sacrament, but its dominant model was rather that of the People of God. This paradigm focused attention on the Church as a network of interpersonal relationships, on the Church as community. This is still the dominant model for many Roman Catholics who consider themselves progressives and invoke the teaching of Vatican II as their authority.

In the postconciliar period still another model of the Church has begun to struggle for supremacy: that of the Church as Servant or Healer. This model is already suggested in some of the later documents of Vatican II, notably the Constitution on the Church in the Modern World (*Gaudium et spes*). This model, with its outgoing thrust, has increased the Catholic Christian's sense of solidarity with the whole human race in its struggles for peace, justice, and prosperity.

As we contemplate the theological history of the Catholic Church over the past thirty years, we cannot but be impressed by the rapidity with which, after a period of long stability, new paradigms have begun to succeed one another. From 1600 to 1940 the juridical or societal model was in peaceful possession, but it was then displaced by that of the Mystical Body, which has been subsequently dislodged by three other models in rapid succession: those of People of God, Sacrament, and Servant. These paradigm shifts closely resemble what Thomas Kuhn has described as "scientific revolutions." But the revolutions he describes have occurred in the pursuit of purely scientific goals. The new scientific paradigms have been accepted because, without sacrificing the good results attained by previous paradigms, they were able in addition to solve problems that had proved intractable by means of the earlier models.

With regard to the ecclesiological revolutions we have mentioned, it seems clear that the new paradigms have in fact cleared up certain problems not easily solved under the predecessors. To a great extent, however, the motives for the shift have been practical and pastoral rather than primarily speculative. Changes have been accepted because they help the Church to find its identity in a changing world, or because they motivate men to the kind of loyalty, commitment, and generosity that the Church seeks to elicit. The People of God image, for example, was adopted in part because it harmonized with the general trend toward democratization in Western society since the eighteenth century. Since Vatican II the Servant Model has become popular because it satisfies a certain hunger for involvement in the making of a better world—a hunger that, although specifically Christian in motivation, establishes solidarity between the Church and the whole human family.

Whatever may be said of the relative merits of the various paradigms, one must recognize that the transition from one to another is fraught with difficulties. Each paradigm brings with it its own favorite set of images, its own rhetoric, its own values, certitudes, commitments, and priorities. It even brings with it a particular set of preferred problems. When paradigms shift, people suddenly find the ground cut out from under their feet. They cannot begin to speak the new language without already committing themselves to a whole new set of values that may not be to their taste. Thus they find themselves gravely threatened in their spiritual security. Theologians, who ought to be able to shift their thinking from one key to another, often resist new paradigms because these eliminate problems on which they have built up a considerable expertise, and introduce other problems with regard to which they have no special competence.

It should not be surprising, therefore, that in the contemporary Church, rocked by paradigm shifts, we should find phenomena such as polarization, mutual incomprehension, inability to communicate, frustration, and discouragement. Since the situation is simply a fact of our times, we must learn to live with it. It will greatly help, however, if people can learn to practice tolerance and to accept pluralism. We must recognize that our own favorite paradigms, however excellent, do not solve all questions. Much harm is done by imperialistically seeking to impose some one model as the definitive one.

Because images are derived from the finite realities of experience, they are never adequate to represent the mystery of grace. Each model of the Church has its weaknesses; no one should be canonized as the measure of all the rest. Instead of searching for some absolutely best image, it would be advisable to recognize that the manifold images given to us by Scripture and Tradition are mutually complementary. They should be made to interpenetrate and mutually qualify one another. None, therefore, should be interpreted in an exclusivistic sense, so as to negate what the other approved models have to teach us. The New Testament, for example, combines the images of Temple and Body of Christ in logically incoherent but theologically apposite ways. In 1 Pet. 2:5 we are told that Christians are a Temple built of living stones, whereas Paul in Eph. 4:16 says that the Body of Christ is still under construction. This "profuse mixing of metaphors," Paul Minear reminds us, "reflects not logical confusion but theological vitality."[20]

In the following chapters an effort will be made to illumine the mystery of the Church through certain dominant models that have become paradigmatic in modern theology. Without attempting to be all-inclusive, I shall concentrate on five such models. In this way I think it will be possible to characterize the leading ecclesiological schools, to identify the most common positions, and to appreciate the internal consistency of various styles of theology. Such a method will present in a clearer light the options that face the theologian, and will show that if he adopts a given model or combination of models, he commits himself in advance to a whole series of positions regarding particular problems.

In the next five chapters the five basic models will be presented with some assessment of their respective strengths and weaknesses. Then in five additional chapters we shall consider how the models lead to diverse positions regarding certain acute problems in contemporary theology. Finally, in a reflective overview, an attempt will be made to summarize the values and limitations of the various models. Although all the models have their merits, they are not of equal worth, and some presentations of some models must positively be rejected.

# The Church as Institution

In Chapter I reference has already been made to the idea that the Church is essentially a society—a "perfect society" in the sense that it is subordinate to no other and lacks nothing required for its own institutional completeness. Bellarmine affirmed that the Church is a society "as visible and palpable as the community of the Roman people, or the Kingdom of France, or the Republic of Venice."[1] The Church is here described by analogies taken from political society.

Insistence on the visibility of the Church has been a standard feature of Roman Catholic ecclesiology from the late Middle Ages until the middle of the present century. On the very eve of Vatican II, Abbot B. C. Butler wrote a book contending that according to Roman Catholics the Church is essentially a single concrete historical society, having "a constitution, a set of rules, a governing body, and a set of actual members who accept this constitution and these rules as binding on them. . . ."[2]

The notion of the Church as society by its very nature tends to highlight the structure of government as the formal element in the society. Thus it leads easily, though not necessarily, to what we shall call in this chapter the institutional vision of the Church—that is to say, the view that defines the Church primarily in terms of its visible structures, especially the rights and powers of its officers.

Institutionalism, as I here define it, is not the same thing as the acceptance of the institutional element in the Church. It will become clear, as our discussion in this book proceeds, that the Church of Christ could not perform its mission without some stable organizational features. It could not unite men of many nations into a well-knit community of conviction, commitment, and hope, and could not minister effectively to the needs of mankind, unless it had responsible officers and properly approved procedures. Throughout its history, from the very earliest years, Christianity has always had an institutional side. It has had recognized ministers, accepted confessional formulas, and prescribed forms of public worship. All this is fitting and proper. It does not necessarily imply institutionalism, any more than papacy implies papalism, or law implies legalism, or dogma implies dogmatism. By institutionalism we mean a system in which the institutional element is treated as primary. From the point of view of this author, institutionalism is a deformation of the true nature of the Church—a deformation that has unfortunately affected the Church at certain periods of its history, and one that remains in every age a real danger to the institutional Church. A Christian believer may energetically oppose institutionalism and still be very much committed to the Church as institution.

Vatican Council II, which for Roman Catholics must count as the most authoritative presentation of ecclesiology in the present century, cannot be fairly accused of institutionalism, though some traces of institutionalism may no doubt be found here and there in the conciliar documents. The primary notions of the Church, in the Dogmatic Constitution *Lumen gentium,* are those of mystery, sacrament, Body of Christ, and People of God. Only after two chapters devoted to these general themes does the Constitution, in its third chapter, proceed to discuss the formal structures of ecclesiastical government. By setting the juridical organization of the Church in the context of a fuller and broader theological consideration of the inner nature of the Church, Vatican II, in my opinion, avoided the pitfalls of juridicism. This is not to say, of course, that the Council solved all the difficulties that may arise in trying to fit together the various aspects of the Church. Surely it left problems unsolved and paved the way for developments it did not achieve. But such limitations are inevitable in the work of any human organization that operates under the conditions of historicity, as even an ecumenical council must do.

As we shall see in later chapters, Catholic theology in the Patristic period and in the Middle Ages, down through the great Scholastic doctors of the thirteenth century, was relatively free of institutionalism. The strongly institutionalist development occurred in the late Middle Ages and the Counter Reformation, when theologians and canonists, responding to attacks on the papacy and hierarchy, accented precisely those features that the adversaries were denying. As Congar remarks, modern Roman Catholic ecclesiology has been marked by a tendency to regard the Church

> as machinery of hierarchical mediation, of the powers and primacy of the Roman see, in a word, "hierarchology." On the other hand, the two terms between which that mediation comes, the Holy Spirit on the one side, the faithful people or the religious subject on the other, were as it were kept out of ecclesiological consideration.[3]

The institutional outlook reached its culmination in the second half of the nineteenth century, and was expressed with singular clarity in the first schema of the Dogmatic Constitution on the Church prepared for Vatican Council I. In a significant paragraph the schema asserted not only that the Church was a perfect society, but that its permanent constitution had been conferred upon it by the Lord himself:

> We teach and declare: The Church has all the marks of a true Society. Christ did not leave this society undefined and without a set form. Rather, he himself gave its existence, and his will determined the form of its existence and gave it its constitution. The Church is not part nor member of any other society and is not min-

gled in any way with any other society. It is so
perfect in itself that it is distinct from all human
societies and stands far above them.[4]

Some of the themes of the Vatican I schema were taken
into the decrees on the papacy adopted by that Council.
Other ideas from the schema were later used by subse-
quent popes—Leo XIII, Pius XI, and Pius XII—in their
encyclicals. Echoes of the Vatican I schema are also found
in the draft constitution on the Church prepared for the
first session of Vatican II.

Because Catholic theology as found in papal documents
and Roman textbooks of the period between Vatican
Councils I and II affords the clearest examples, we shall in
this chapter take most of our examples of institutionalism
from these sources. Although there are exaggerations in
this theology, we do not wish to be understood as suggest-
ing that every position taken by the institutionalists was
wrong. Because we are here expounding only one type of
ecclesiology, we shall have to leave open the question how
far the claims of institutionalism would have to be moder-
ated in a balanced ecclesiology that draws on various
models, giving the institution no more—and no less—than
its due.

In the institutionalist ecclesiology the powers and functions of the Church are generally divided into three:
teaching, sanctifying, and governing. This division of
powers leads to further distinctions between the Church
teaching and the Church taught, the Church sanctifying
and the Church sanctified, the Church governing and the
Church governed. In each case the Church as institution
is on the giving end. So these authors say: The Church
teaches, sanctifies, and commands, in each case identifying
the Church itself with the governing body or hierarchy.

When viewed according to each of these respective
functions, the Church has somewhat different analogates
in the secular order. From the point of view of its teaching
function, it resembles a school in which the masters, as sacred teachers, hand down the doctrine of Christ. Because

the bishops are considered to possess a special "charism of truth" (the phrase is from St. Irenaeus, but the meaning has undergone a change since his time),[5] it is held that the faithful are in conscience bound to believe what the bishops declare. The Church is therefore a unique type of school—one in which the teachers have the power to impose their doctrine with juridical and spiritual sanctions. Thus teaching is juridicized and institutionalized.

The same is true of the second function, that of sanctifying. Some authors speak almost as though sanctity were a kind of substance inherent in the Church. The pope and bishops, assisted by priests and deacons, are described somewhat as if they were engineers opening and shutting the valves of grace.

The third function, government, is likewise in the hands of the hierarchy. There is one difference, however. Whereas in teaching and sanctifying, the hierarchy have a merely ministerial function, transmitting the doctrine and grace of Christ himself, ruling is something that they do in their own name. They govern the flock with pastoral authority, and as Christ's viceregents impose new laws and precepts under pain of sin.

A characteristic of the institutional model of the Church, in the forms we are considering, is the hierarchical conception of authority. The Church is not conceived as a democratic or representative society, but as one in which the fullness of power is concentrated in the hands of a ruling class that perpetuates itself by cooption. This vision is clearly set forth in the Vatican I schema:

> But the Church of Christ is not a community of equals in which all the faithful have the same rights. It is a society of unequals, not only because among the faithful some are clerics and some are laymen, but particularly because there is in the Church the power from God whereby to some it is given to sanctify, teach, and govern, and to others not.[6]

At the first session of Vatican II, Bishop Emile De Smedt of Bruges characterized the preliminary schema by three terms that have since become famous: clericalism, juridicism, and triumphalism.[7] These terms are applicable to the ecclesiology we have been considering. It is, in the first place, clericalist, for it views the clergy, especially the higher clergy, as the source of all power and initiative. Bishop De Smedt spoke of the pyramidal pattern in which all power is conceived as descending from the pope through the bishops and priests, while at the base the faithful people play a passive role and seem to have a lower position in the Church. In contrast to this view, the bishop reminded the conciliar Fathers that in the Church all have the same fundamental rights and duties, so that popes and bishops, together with lay persons, are to be reckoned among the faithful people of God.

Secondly, this view is juridicist, for it conceives of authority in the Church rather closely on the pattern of jurisdiction in the secular state, and greatly amplifies the place of law and penalties. There is a tendency to juridicize not only the ruling power, but even the powers of teaching and sanctifying, so that spiritual ministries are not regarded as effective unless they conform to the prescriptions of canon law. Bishop De Smedt particularly criticized the juridical approach to the question of membership, and called for a manner of speaking and thinking that exhibited the Church as being, in the term used by Pope John XXIII, "the loving mother of all."

Finally, this ecclesiology is triumphalistic. It dramatizes the Church as an army set in array against Satan and the powers of evil. Such phrases, said Bishop De Smedt, are scarcely in keeping with the condition of the People of God as a "little flock" following the humble Lord Jesus.

Operating in terms of a world view in which everything remains essentially the same as it was when it began, and in which origins are therefore all-important, the institutionalist ecclesiology attaches crucial importance to the action of Christ in establishing the offices and sacraments that presently exist in the Church. Thus the Council of

Trent taught that the seven sacraments, and a hierarchy consisting of bishops, priests, and ministers, were instituted by Christ.[8] Vatican I affirmed the same of the papal office.[9] By the same logic, the dogmas of the modern Church were affirmed to be part of the original deposit of faith, complete with the apostles.[10]

As it became increasingly clear that scholarly criticism could not demonstrate that all these offices, beliefs, and rites were instituted by Christ, theologians were urged to study the original sources using what is called the "regressive method"[11]—i.e., utilizing the latest teaching of the magisterium as an indication of what must have been present from the beginning, since the Church at this period disclaimed any power of innovation in its teaching of revelation. In this conception, "the noblest office of theology" was thought to be, in the phrase used by Pius IX and Pius XII, "to show how a doctrine defined by the Church is contained in the sources of Revelation."[12] Theology itself was thus drawn into the institutionalism of which we have been speaking. The theologian's tasks of appraising the current teaching of the magisterium, and of preparing the way for new doctrinal development, were slighted in favor of his role of defending what the magisterium had already said.

To clarify the institutional model somewhat further, it will be helpful to explain how this theory would conceive of the bonds that unify the Church, the beneficiaries that are served by the Church, and the nature of the benefits bestowed by the Church.

The bonds are basically the same as the three mentioned by Robert Bellarmine, as explained in the previous chapter. The members of the Church are those who profess the approved doctrines, communicate in the legitimate sacraments, and who subject themselves to the duly appointed pastors. In the words of *Mystici corporis*: "Only those are really (*reapse*) to be included as members of the Church who have been baptized and profess the true faith and who have not unhappily withdrawn from the Body-unity or who for grave faults have been excluded by legitimate authority."[13]

For the institutional model it is crucially important that all the tests of membership be visible, that is to say, juridically applicable. Thus this theory, by its inner logic, tends to resist notions of "invisible membership," which are quite tolerable in some of the theories to which we shall turn in later chapters.

The beneficiaries of the Church, in the institutional model, are its own members. The Church is the school that instructs them regarding the truths they need to know for the sake of their eternal salvation. It is the refectory or inn where they are nourished from the life-giving streams of grace, which flows especially through the sacraments. It is the hospital where they are healed of their illnesses, the shelter where they are protected against the assaults of the enemy of their souls. Thanks to the governing authority of the shepherds, the faithful are kept from wandering into the desert and are led to the green pastures.

From all this it is clear what the Church does for its beneficiaries: It gives them eternal life. The Church is compared to a loving mother who nourishes her infants at the breast, or, more impersonally, to the boat of Peter, which carries the faithful to the farther shore of heaven, provided they remain on board. They have only to be docile and obedient, and to rely on the ministrations of the Church. According to Cyprian, "He cannot have God for his Father who does not have the Church for his mother."[14] According to the Vatican I schema, "It is an article of faith that outside the Church no one can be saved. . . . Who is not in this ark will perish in the flood."[15] Subtle distinctions are made to mitigate the apparently harsh consequences of this position without lessening the motivation to join and remain in the "true Church."

In saying that the Church, so conceived, exists for the benefit of its own members, I do not wish to imply that it is indifferent regarding the eternal destiny of the rest of men. On the contrary, the institutional model gives strong support to the missionary effort by which the Church goes out to nonmembers. But it seeks to save their souls precisely by bringing them into the institution. For the proverbial old-style missionary—who is not a totally mythical figure—success is statistically measurable: How many baptisms have been performed, how many persons have entered the Church, how many continue to come regularly to church and receive the sacraments?

In order to avoid anticipating points to be made later in connection with other models, I have concentrated in this chapter on highly institutional views, especially those found in Roman Catholicism from about 1550 to 1950. In this theology the Church tends to become a *total* institution—one that exists for its own sake and serves others only by aggrandizing itself. More moderately institutional views make room for other aspects of the Church that have yet to be considered.

What are the chief assets of this strong institutionalism? They are, in my opinion, three. In the first place, the theory has strong endorsement in official Church documents of the past few centuries. Since the Catholic Church repeatedly affirms that its doctrinal, sacramental, and governmental structures are founded in divine revelation, it is difficult for the faithful to take a different position. Any Catholic who wants to back away from these institutional claims is likely to be embarrassed by the strong official pronouncements that can be quoted against him.

Secondly, the institutional approach, by insisting strongly on the element of continuity with Christian origins, provides important links between an uncertain present and an esteemed religious past. In a time when many are suffering from future shock, it is no small asset for the Church to be able to provide a zone of stability in a world that gyrates madly from extreme to extreme.

Finally, the institutional model has in recent centuries served to give Roman Catholics a strong sense of corporate identity. They knew clearly who they were and what they stood for, when they were succeeding and when they were failing. They had a high degree of institutional loyalty, since they were strongly motivated to accept the declared aims and teachings of the Church. The Church had clear goals for missionary action, and was vexed by a minimum of internal dissent. Other Christians frequently envied Catholics for their *esprit de corps.*

On the other hand, the institutional theory labors under several major liabilities. The case against it may be summarized as follows. In the first place, the theory has a comparatively meager basis in Scripture and in early Church tradition. It can claim support only from a very few New Testament texts, and even these must be interpreted in a particular prescribed way. In point of fact, Scripture does not portray the Church as a single tightly knit society. As we shall see in later chapters, Paul's models of the Church tend to be more organic, more communitarian, more mystical.

Secondly, the institutional model leads to some unfortunate consequences in Christian life, both personal and corporate. While some virtues, such as obedience, are strongly accented, others are not. The deficiencies of the theory may be conveniently summarized under the three terms we have quoted from Bishop De Smedt. Clericalism tends to reduce the laity to a condition of passivity, and to make their apostolate a mere appendage of the apostolate of the hierarchy—a view endorsed by Pius XI and Pius XII in their descriptions of "Catholic action."[16] Juridicism tends to exaggerate the role of human authority and thus to turn the gospel into a new law. Catholics in the Counter Reformation period became overly concerned with fulfilling ecclesiastical obligations and insufficiently attentive, at times, to fulfilling the law of charity. Concerned with maintaining the right relationships with pope and bishops, they attended less than they should to God, to Christ, and to the Holy Spirit.

In comparison with the institutional model, the biblical sources seem to place the accent far more on the prophetic. Jesus was highly critical of the institutional religion of his day, and he based his authority not on any institutional appointment or office but on the Spirit by which he spoke. Paul's ecclesiology gives a major place to non-official charisms. On a biblical basis one may conclude that Christianity is not healthy unless there is room in it for prophetic protest against abuses of authority. Protest would lose its power if it always had to capitulate in the face of threats of ecclesiastical censure.

A third difficulty against the institutional model is that it raises obstacles to a creative and fruitful theology. According to some critics it binds theology too exclusively to the defense of currently official positions, and thus diminishes critical and exploratory thinking.

Fourthly, exaggerated institutionalism leads to many serious theological problems, some of which have already been intimated. For example, the theologian is asked to find in Scripture and apostolic tradition things that honest scholarship can scarcely find in them—such as the papal-episcopal form of government, the seven sacraments, and modern dogmas such as the Immaculate Conception and the Assumption. In some presentations of this ecclesiology it seems enormously difficult to admit the salvation of non-Roman Catholics—and yet the idea that most of mankind would be eternally damned for not being Catholics is incredible and theologically intolerable. Ecumenically, this ecclesiology is sterile. As will be seen in a later chapter, the institutional model fails to account for the spiritual vitality of non-Roman Catholic churches. And within the Roman Catholic Church, this ecclesiology fails to give sufficient scope to the charismatic element. The gifts and graces of the Holy Spirit, it would seem, must wait upon the approbation of the official leadership.

Finally, this ecclesiology is out of phase with the demands of the times. In an age of dialogue, ecumenism, and interest in world religions, the monopolistic tendencies of this model are unacceptable. In an age when all large institutions are regarded with suspicion or aversion, it is exceptionally difficult to attract people to a religion that represents itself as primarily institutional. As sociologists have noted, we are experiencing in our age the breakdown of closed societies.[17] While people are willing to dedicate themselves to a cause or a movement, they do not wish to bind themselves totally to any institution. Institutions are seen as self-serving and repressive and as needing to be kept under strong vigilance. In our modern pluralistic society, especially in a country such as the United States, people do not experience any given church as a necessary means of giving significance to their lives, but they may prefer a certain church as providing specific services that could not be equally well obtained elsewhere. Fulfillment and significance are things that an individual usually finds more in the private than in the public sphere, more in the personal than in the institutional.

In every generation the Church has to face anew the problem of how to maintain its institutional strength and societal stability without falling into the defects of exaggerated institutionalism. If we work from the notion of the Church as mystery, as outlined in Chapter I, we shall have a means of keeping institutionalism within proper bounds. We shall see that the Church is not primarily institution; that it does not derive all its reality and strength from its institutional features. The institutional elements in the Church must ultimately be justified by their capacity to express or strengthen the Church as a community of life, witness, and service, a community that reconciles and unites men in the grace of Christ.

In spite of the overemphasis on the institutional in official Roman Catholic theology, especially since the Reformation, the institutional model of the Church has rarely been advocated in its purity. Even the schema of Vatican I and the encyclicals of Leo XIII and Pius XII, for all their insistence on the Church as a "perfect society," never identified the society exclusively with its institutional elements. They tempered the institutional with more spiritual and organic conceptions, such as those of the communion of grace or the Body of Christ. For a fuller understanding of moderate institutionalism, therefore, one must draw upon the communitarian and mystical views of the Church, to which we shall now turn our attention.

# III

# The Church as Mystical Communion

In modern sociology it has become commonplace to contrast two types of social relationship: a formally organized or structured society, and an informal or interpersonal community. The two types are often referred to by their German names, *Gesellschaft* (society) and *Gemeinschaft* (community).[1] *Gesellschaft*, in this categorization, corresponds approximately with the kinds of grouping we have analyzed in the preceding chapter under the headings of institution and visible society. It is a human association characterized by formal organization, structures, and office, such as the secular state, the school, the hospital, the hotel. The organization is maintained by competent authority, which is normally institutionalized in the form of office. Such societies are governed by explicit rules, often written.

Since the institutional categories, as we have seen, cannot do justice to the full reality of the Church, it is to be expected that theologians would turn to the other member of the pair to illuminate the nature of the Church. The notion of *Gemeinschaft*, in Tönnies' classification, was further developed by Charles H. Cooley in his description of "primary groups."[2] The chief characteristics of a primary group, as he explains, are five: (1) face-to-face association; (2) the unspecialized character of that association; (3) relative permanence; (4) the small number of persons involved; (5) the relative intimacy among the participants.[3]

As examples of primary groups, Cooley referred to the family, the household, and the old-fashioned neighborhood. Such groups, he explained, are primary chiefly in the sense that they are fundamental in forming the social nature of the individual.

> The result of intimate association, psychologically, is a certain fusion of individualities in a common whole, so that one's very self, for many purposes at least, is the common life and purpose of the group. Perhaps the simplest way of describing the wholeness is by saying that it is a "we"; it involves the sort of sympathy and mutual identification for which "we" is the natural expression. One lives in the feeling of the whole and finds the chief aims of his will in that feeling.[4]

The notion of the Church as community has appealed to many modern theologians. In some Protestant circles, this notion has been developed in an anti-institutional sense. Rudolph Sohm, for instance, taught that the essential nature of the Church stands in antithesis to all law.[5] Emil Brunner, in *The Misunderstanding of the Church*, argued that the Church in the biblical sense (the *Ecclesia*) is not an institution but a brotherhood (*Bruderschaft*); it is "a pure communion of persons (*Personengemeinschaft*)."[6] On this ground Brunner rejected all law, sacrament, and priestly office as incompatible with the true being of the Church.

Without drawing these negative conclusions, Dietrich Bonhoeffer developed the notion of the Church as an interpersonal community. In his first major theological work, *The Communion of Saints*, he wrote: "The community is constituted by the complete self-forgetfulness of love. The relationship between I and thou is no longer essentially a demanding but a giving one."[7]

In Roman Catholic ecclesiology, the Church was studied in terms of Tönnies' categories in Arnold Rademacher's *Die Kirche als Gemeinschaft und Gesellschaft*.[8] Rademacher maintains that the Church is in its inner core community (*Gemeinschaft*); in its outer core, however, it is society (*Gesellschaft*). The society is the outward manifestation of the community; and the society exists in order to promote the realization of the community. The community is the "real," as contrasted with the phenomenal, Church; it coincides with the Kingdom of God and with the Communion of Saints.

In French-speaking Roman Catholicism, the Dominicans Yves Congar and Jérôme Hamer have made the category of community or communion central to their ecclesiology. Throughout the works of Congar one encounters the idea that the Church has two inseparable aspects. On the one hand it is a fellowship of persons—a fellowship of men with God and with one another in Christ. On the other hand the Church is also the totality of the means by which this fellowship is produced and maintained. In its former aspect the Church is *Heilsgemeinschaft* (community of salvation); in its latter aspect, *Heilsanstalt* (institution of salvation). In its ultimate reality, Congar says, the Church is a fellowship of persons.[9]

Hamer rejects on the one hand Bellarmine's definition that would characterize the Church only in terms of its external, institutional features, and on the other hand the view of Sohm and Brunner that would see the institutional as illegitimate. Maintaining with Congar that both aspects are essential, he seeks to combine them under the notion of communion. The Church, he concludes, "the mystical body of Christ, is a communion which is at once inward and external, an inner communion of spiritual life (of faith, hope, and charity) signified and engendered by an external communion in profession of the faith, discipline and the sacramental life."[10]

In characterizing the Church as communion Hamer does not mean that it is simply a community in the sociological sense (primary group, as described above). He distinguishes within the notion of communion between the horizontal and the vertical dimensions. Communion in the sense of sociological group would be simply horizontal; it would be a matter of friendly relationships between man and man. What is distinctive to the Church, he maintains, is the vertical dimension—the divine life disclosed in the incarnate Christ and communicated to men through his Spirit. The outward and visible bonds of a brotherly society are an element in the reality of the Church, but they rest upon a deeper spiritual communion of grace or charity. The communion given by the Holy Spirit finds expression in a network of mutual interpersonal relationships of concern and assistance.[11]

The concept of the Church as a communion harmonizes with several biblical images—most notably with two images that have figured prominently in modern Catholic ecclesiology, as summarized in Chapter I: those of the Body of Christ and the People of God. These two images, after a long period of neglect in Catholic theology, returned to favor in the present century. The groundwork for this revival was laid in the nineteenth century by Johann Adam Möhler and his associates in the Tübingen school. Reacting against the aridity of the institutional models, they popularized the notion of the Church as a supernatural organism vivified by the Holy Spirit, a fellowship sustained by the outpouring of divine grace.

The image of the Body of Christ is organic, rather than sociological. The Church is seen on the analogy of a human body equipped with various organs. It has an inbuilt vital principle thanks to which it can grow, repair itself, and adapt itself to changing needs. The Body of Christ, as distinct from any natural organism, has a divine life-principle. On most explanations this is said to be the Holy Spirit.

The idea of the Church as Body of Christ is found in Paul. In Rom. 12 and 1 Cor. 12 the main point is the mutual union, mutual concern, and mutual dependence of the members of the local community upon one another. No mention is made in these epistles of Christ as head, still less of the Holy Spirit as soul. In Ephesians and Colossians, on the other hand, the accent is on the headship of Christ and on the subordination of the total Church to him.[12]

Many of the Church Fathers, including Augustine,[13] develop the image of the Body of Christ with particular stress on the mystical and invisible communion that binds together all those who are enlivened by the grace of Christ. Augustine speaks of a Church that includes not only the earthly but the heavenly: The angels and the blessed are members of the heavenly part of the Church. Christ as head makes up one totality together with all his members. The Body is not essentially visible, since it includes angels and separated souls. Still less is it societal, since it includes all men who are animated by the spirit of God. All the just from Abel on are in the Body of Christ, in the *Ecclesia ab Abel*. Augustine already has the idea of the Holy Spirit as soul of the body.

In the High Middle Ages doctors such as Thomas Aquinas[14] begin to sketch the rudiments of a treatise on the Church in their reflections on Christ as head of all the redeemed. For Aquinas the Church essentially consists in a divinizing communion with God, whether incompletely in this life or completely in the life of glory. The grace that is the seed of glory is the grace of Christ, and hence the Church is made up of all who are brought into union with God by supernatural grace flowing from Christ as head. Aquinas' view of the Church is "theologal" rather than institutional. The Body of Christ for him is not essentially visible or societal, still less hierarchical.

The Holy Spirit comes indirectly into Aquinas' notion of the Church as the principle of unity that dwells in Christ and in us, binding together with him and in him. Aquinas uses the category of instrumental causality to show how the humanity of Christ and the sacraments can be communicators of the grace of God. All the external means of grace (sacraments, scripture, laws, etc.) are secondary and subordinate; their role is simply to dispose men for an interior union with God effected by grace.

After a period of strong institutionalism in ecclesiology, the theology of the Church as Mystical Body began to revive in the middle of the nineteenth century. In the early twentieth century ecclesiology was revitalized by a return to biblical and patristic sources. In this period the Belgian Jesuit Emile Mersch devoted his life to restoring the notion of the Mystical Body as the key concept of theology. He made a distinction between the Church, as "the society of baptized believers under the direction of its legitimate shepherds," and the Mystical Body as "The Unity of those who live with the life of Christ."[15]

There were in this period some rather exaggerated developments of Mystical Body theology.[16] Karl Pelz, in *Der Christ als Christus* (1939), held that the hypostatic union is in some way extended to all Christians. Also during this period there were many attacks on the idea of the Mystical Body as being too vague and biological to serve as a definition of the Church.

In 1943 Pius XII published his famous encyclical in which, as we have seen, he defined the Church of Jesus Christ as the Mystical Body of Christ, and stated that the Mystical Body is identical with the Roman Catholic Church. This encyclical attempts to harmonize the "Mystical Body" concept with the societal concept of Bellarmine. It points to the pope and the bishops as the joints and ligaments of the body, and asserts that "those who exercise sacred power in the Body are its first and chief members." The laity are said to "assist the ecclesiastical hierarchy in spreading the Kingdom of the divine Redeemer" and thus to occupy an honorable, even though often lowly, place in the Christian community.[17]

Vatican II in *Lumen gentium*[18] reaffirms the idea that the Church is the Body of Christ, but it slightly retrenches from two positions taken by *Mystici corporis*. It distinguishes between the Church as hierarchical society and as Body of Christ, and asserts that the two are related to each other in a way comparable to the human and divine natures of Christ. The structure of the Church is described as an instrument serving Christ's Spirit, who vivifies it in building up his Body. Secondly, *Lumen gentium* does not assert that the Church of Christ or the Mystical Body is coterminous with the Roman Catholic Church.[19]

The principal paradigm of the Church in the documents of Vatican II is that of the People of God. The People of God is a biblical concept having deep roots in the Old Testament, where Israel is constantly referred to as the nation of God's special predilection. In several New Testament texts (Rom. 9:23–26, Heb. 8:10, James 1:1, 1 Pt. 2:9, etc.) the Christian Ekklesia is referred to as the new Israel or as the People of God of the New Covenant. In the second chapter of the Vatican II Constitution on the Church, the new People of God is described as a Spirit-filled community, "a fellowship of life, charity, and truth." While this People is said to be "equipped with those means which befit it as a visible and social unity,"[20] it is not exclusively identified with any given societal organization, even the Roman Catholic Church. The People of God is coextensive with the Body of Christ.

For many purposes the analogues of Body of Christ and People of God are virtually equivalent. Both of them are more democratic in tendency than the hierarchical models that we have seen in our second chapter. They emphasize the immediate relationship of all believers to the Holy Spirit, who directs the whole Church. Both focus attention likewise on the mutual service of the members toward one another and on the subordination of the particular good of any one group to that of the whole Body or People.

The image of the People of God, however, differs from that of the Body of Christ in that it allows for a greater distance between the Church and its divine head. The Church is seen as a community of persons each of whom is individually free. In stressing the continual mercy of God and the continual need of the Church for repentance, the People of God model picks up many favorite themes of Protestant theology, themes that can be at home in Roman Catholicism, as *Lumen gentium* proves when it speaks of the Church as both holy and sinful, as needing repentance and reform.[21]

The image of the People of God has certain weaknesses. Congar[22] points out that it fails to bring out as clearly as

"Body of Christ" what is new in the New Covenant,
namely that men are brought into a consciously affirmed
filial relationship to God. We become by adoption what
Jesus Christ is by origin: sons of God. In many authors,
not exclusively Protestant, one gets the impression that we
are still living pretty much under the conditions of the
Old Law. The abiding presence of the Holy Spirit is capable of being integrated with the concept of the People of
God, especially if this is developed along the lines of the
"new covenant" written on men's hearts (Jer. 31:33); but
the uniqueness of the Church of Christ is better conveyed
by the term "Body of Christ."

The term "People of God," when used as a synonym for
the Church, strikes many as egotistical and monopolistic.
How can any particular group of men affirm that they,
and they alone, are God's own people? Actually, the Bible
itself testifies (Gen. 8–9) that God has entered into a
covenant-relationship with all mankind, and thus that all
men are in some sort members of the People of God. The
Church, or the Christian community, might better be
designated as the "People of God of the New Covenant"—
a covenant that completes and makes explicit the relationship of fidelity and love into which God has entered
with mankind thanks to his beloved Son, Jesus Christ.
Christians are set apart by their explicit recognition of the
new and everlasting Covenant, but they are not uniquely
the People of God.

There is a sense in which the notion of People of God,
like that of Body of Christ, is metaphorical. The root of
the metaphor is the kind of treaty relationship into which
a suzerain state entered with a vassal state in the ancient
Near East. That kind of military and political treaty
afforded the raw material out of which the concept of
"People of God" was fashioned.

We have indicated several reasons why the image of
Body of Christ is superior to that of People of God. But
this image too has its defects. As indicated in our historical summary, the notion of Body of Christ has been
variously understood in different periods of history. Re-

garding the modern concept of "Mystical Body," it will have to be asked: Is this body a pure communion of grace, or is it essentially visible? If the former, it does not seem to be identical with the Church of Christ, which is usually understood as a community of Christian believers, bound together by bonds of explicit faith, worship, and ecclesiastical fellowship. If the latter, is there not need for another term to designate the invisible communion of grace which for Augustine and Thomas would seem to be the essence of the Body of Christ?

Further, the designation of the Church as Body of Christ is in danger of leading to an unhealthy divinization of the Church. It seems to suggest the erroneous position of Pelz that the Church is one organism together with its head, and that the union is therefore a biological and hypostatic one. If the Holy Spirit were conceived as the life principle of the Church, all the actions of the Church would seem to be attributable to the Holy Spirit. This would obscure the personal responsibility and freedom of the members, and would make the presence of sin and error in the Church—even on the corporate and official level—unintelligible. The notion of People of God is from this point of view preferable; it better respects the concrete reality of the Church as a human grouping in history.

In sum, the two models of Body of Christ and People of God both illuminate from different angles the notion of the Church as communion or community. The Church, from this point of view, is not in the first instance an institution or a visibly organized society. Rather it is a communion of men, primarily interior but also expressed by external bonds of creed, worship, and ecclesiastical fellowship.

The relationship between the Church and the Holy Spirit, prominent in the models of the People of God and the Body of Christ, is exhaustively explored in the recent ecclesiological writings of Heribert Mühlen.[23] Mühlen's work is far too monumental to be summarized here. He recognizes, as we do, that the notions of People of God

and Body of Christ are basically metaphors. Taken in isolation, he says, they lead respectively to the contrary errors
of sociologism and biologism. He believes that it is possible to get beyond metaphor by attending to the interpersonal nature of the Church. The mutual union of persons
without loss of their distinctness, he further contends, is
properly the work of the Holy Spirit, who in the godhead
is one person in many persons. So with regard to mankind,
the Holy Spirit is the divine person who makes us one
without our ceasing to be many. The Church is one Person (the Holy Spirit) in many persons (Christ and us).
The union of the members with one another and with
Christ is neither organic on the one hand nor merely
moral or juridical on the other; rather it is a new type of
union that Mühlen describes as "personalogical." The
union is both an interior sanctificatory union—taking place
in the inmost personal core of the members—and a visible
consecratory union—sealed by office and sacraments.

Mühlen's work is a major advance over those ecclesiologies that seek to work exclusively in terms of either juridical or biological models. In many ways, his is the most important Catholic contribution to systematic ecclesiology
since Vatican II. Inverting the usual procedure, he begins
with the Trinitarian processions and argues deductively to
the missions of the Son and the Holy Spirit and to their
roles with respect to the Church. In this way Mühlen
gives the impression of relying less than others do on the
data of experience. But in point of fact it could be shown,
I think, that the very notions of person and procession
with which he begins are founded upon the experience of
Christians in the Church. Many key terms in his analysis,
such as "sanctificatory union" and "consecratory union,"
are "analogue models" rising scarcely above the level of
sheer metaphor. Thus Mühlen falls short of his goal of a
fully systematic ecclesiology elaborated in metaphysical
terms. Like other theologians, he depends on concepts
drawn from the observable order and applied to God by
an "analogy of faith."

Other Catholic writers, since Vatican II, have turned

more to the sociological concept of community as a principle for the renewal of the Church.[24] They would wish to
see the Church in our time become a place in which one
can establish rich and satisfying primary relationships—
that is, person-to-person relationships founded on mutual
understanding and love. The Church, according to this
view, is a great community made up of many interlocking
communities. Thanks to the unifying presence of the Holy
Spirit, the many families of Christians are woven into a
single large family.

In this chapter we have surveyed a variety of ecclesiological models that have as their common factor the emphasis on the communion of the members with one another
and with God in Christ. To appreciate the difference between these communion ecclesiologies and the institutional ecclesiologies previously studied, we may ask the
same three questions put to the institutional: What are
the bonds of union? Who are the beneficiaries? What is
the goal or purpose of the Church?

The bonds of union, in these theories, would be primarily the interior graces and gifts of the Holy Spirit, though
the external bonds are recognized as important in a sub-
sidiary way. The resulting union would surpass anything
known to pure sociology; it would be a transforming mystical union, deeper and more intimate than anything de-
scribable in moral or juridical terms. The term "member"
may still be used, but in this ecclesiology it is no longer a
juridical term. Rather it is used in an organic, spiritual, or
mystical sense, referring to the Church as a communion of
grace. The primary factor that binds the members of the
Church to each other is the reconciling grace of Christ. In
some presentations this implies a doctrine of invisible
membership. All who are made friends by the grace of
Christ, in this view, would in some sense be members of
the People of God or the Body of Christ.

Who, then, are the beneficiaries of the Church? As in
the first model, so here too, the members are the
beneficiaries. But the members are understood in a more
spiritual sense, as those animated by supernatural faith

and charity. The maxim "outside the Church no salvation," which in the first model appeared as institutional triumphalism, becomes in this model almost a tautology.

The goal of the Church, in this second ecclesiological type, is a spiritual or supernatural one. The Church aims to lead men into communion with the divine. But that goal is not simply the reward of a life well lived. To some extent it is given with the very existence of the Church. Wherever the Church is present, men are already united with God. In the oft-quoted phrase of Irenaeus, "Where the Spirit of God is, there is the Church and every grace."[25] The Church is not a mere means. It is not just a vehicle to bring men to heaven. The Church in a certain sense exists for its own sake. Wherever men are in the Church they have partly fulfilled the aim of their existence; they are, at least inchoatively, in union with God.

Some evaluative remarks are now in order. In many respects the communion model is an improvement over that which sees the Church primarily as institution. This type of ecclesiology has a better basis in the biblical notion of communion (*koinonia*) as found in the Book of Acts and in the Pauline descriptions of the Church as the Body of Christ. It picks up the biblical theme that God has fashioned for himself a people by freely communicating his Spirit and his gifts. The approach is ecumenically very fruitful, for the themes of the Body of Christ and the People of God are far more congenial to most Protestants and Orthodox than the institutional model set forth in the last chapter. As already pointed out, the notion of "People of God," if not interpreted in an exclusivistic way, could open up a path to dialogue with Jews and with other major religions.

Also on the credit side is the fact that the communion ecclesiologies have an excellent foundation in the Catholic tradition. The notion of communion was a central theme in the early Christian centuries.[26] The great doctors of the Church, including Augustine and Aquinas, develop their ecclesiologies primarily from their doctrine of grace as a communal gift. Communion-type ecclesiologies, moreover, agree well with the highest doctrinal teaching of the Church in the past generation. Pius XII made the theme of the Body of Christ central to the official ecclesiology of his day, and Vatican II has deliberately subordinated the theme of hierarchical office, which loomed so large in nineteenth-century documents, to the concept of the Church as People of God.

Thirdly, this type of ecclesiology, by accenting the personal relationship between the faithful—individually and collectively—with the Holy Spirit, helps to revivify spirituality and the life of prayer. It makes room for the spontaneous initiatives aroused by the Holy Spirit, who gives to each according to his good pleasure without prior consultation with the hierarchy. In pointing up the ecclesial value of informal, spontaneous, interpersonal relationships within the Church, this model does much to restore the warm and vital interrelationships so central to the New Testament vision of the Church.

Finally, these interpersonal models have great appeal in our day because they meet a human need that is acutely experienced by many of the faithful. As pointed out in the evaluation of institutionalism at the close of the second chapter, large institutions are accepted as at best a necessary evil. They are felt to be oppressive and depersonalizing. People find the meaning of their lives not in terms of such institutions but in terms of the informal, the personal, the communal. They long for a community which, in spite of all the conflicts built into modern society, can open up loving communication. The Church, if it can perform this function, will be enthusiastically welcomed.

Notwithstanding their many advantages, these communal types of ecclesiology suffer from certain weaknesses. For one thing, they leave some obscurity regarding the relationships between the spiritual and visible dimensions of the Church. If the Church is seen totally as a free and spontaneous gift of the Spirit, the organizational and hierarchical aspect of the Church runs the risk of appearing superfluous. There is a danger of falling into a kind of dualism, as Emil Brunner does when he contrasts the

*Ekklesia* of personalism with the Church of law and order, and as Paul Tillich does when he contrasts the "Spiritual Community" with the churches.[27] Official Roman Catholic teaching, in our view, does well to stress the divine value of both the organizational and the communal aspects of the Church and their mutual complementarity. But the communion ecclesiology does not by itself provide any basis for a convincing answer to the arguments of a Brunner or a Tillich, who would separate the visible from the spiritual, and look upon the latter alone as the properly divine or religious element.

A second difficulty in this model is that, as generally explained, it tends to exalt and divinize the Church beyond its due. We have already seen how this is the case with the notion of the Body of Christ, which apprehends the Church in terms of the Incarnation. The same is true of the People of God, if this entity is viewed as coterminous with the Christian Church. In our day, when efforts are being made to enter into respectful dialogue with other faiths, these claims are often felt to be an embarrassment.

Thirdly, this type of ecclesiology fails to give Christians a very clear sense of their identity or mission. Since we cannot take it for granted that evangelization, baptism, or church membership coincides with the bestowal of the Holy Spirit, the motivation for Christian mission is left obscure.

Finally, there is built into these ecclesiologies a certain tension between the Church as a network of friendly interpersonal relationships and the Church as a mystical communion of grace. The term *koinonia* (communion) is used ambiguously to cover both, but it is not evident that the two necessarily go together. Is the Church more importantly a friendly fellowship among men or a mystical communion that has its basis in God? The former view, prevalent in some forms of Protestantism, tends to fragment the Church into a multitude of autonomous congregations; the latter, more prominent in Eastern monasticism, seems to endorse a kind of flight into mystical interiority. Many Christian theologians, including Catholics such as Congar, Hamer, and Mühlen, try to combine both concepts as two dimensions of a single reality. But it is not clear that outgoing friendliness in point of fact leads to the most intense experience of God. For some persons, perhaps, it does, but not for all.[28]

In many instances, the effort to find a perfect interpersonal communion in the Church has led to frustration if not to apostasy. While the Church promises communion, it does not always provide it in very evident form. Christians commonly experience the Church more as a companionship of fellow travelers on the same journey than as a union of lovers dwelling in the same home. Gregory Baum expresses some wise reservations about the tendency of some Catholics to drift into underground churches in the hope of finding some more ideal type of community:

> Some people involved in the underground are eagerly looking for the perfect human community. They long for a community which fulfills all their needs and in terms of which they are able to define themselves. This search is illusory, especially in our own day when to be human means to participate in several communities and to remain critical in regard to all of them. The longing desire for the warm and understanding total community is the search for the good mother, which is bound to end in disappointment and heartbreak. There are no good mothers and fathers, there is only the divine mystery summoning and freeing us to grow up.[29]

Baum here sounds a note of sober realism that should be taken to heart by overenthusiastic proponents of underground churches and of "basic Christian communities." Yet cynicism should not have the last word. Christians are obliged to strive unceasingly to build better and more Christlike communities on all levels, from the family circle to the United Nations. Some Christians—and not merely those who join religious orders—will be privileged to live in basic communities in which their ordinary human relationships are healed and enriched by a common commitment to Christ and the gospel. Communities of this type are, in a very important sense, realizations of the Church.

# IV

# The Church as Sacrament

In the past two chapters we have noted a certain tension between the institutional and the mystical visions of the Church. The institutional model seems to deny salvation to anyone who is not a member of the organization, whereas the communion model leaves it problematical why anyone should be required to join the institution at all. In order to bring together the external and internal aspects into some intelligible synthesis, many twentieth-century Catholic theologians have appealed to the concept of the Church as sacrament. Anticipated by Cyprian, Augustine, Aquinas, and Scheeben, this type of ecclesiology emerged in full clarity in our own century.[1]

On the basis of an extraordinary familiarity with the patristic and medieval sources, Henri de Lubac made a major contribution to this theory. The divine and the human in the Church, he argued, can never be dissociated. An excessively spiritual and individualistic view of the life of grace, he maintained, leads to a merely secular and sociological understanding of the Church as institution. The notion of sacrament, on the other hand, harmoniously combines both aspects.

> If Christ is the sacrament of God, the Church is for us the sacrament of Christ; she represents him, in the full and ancient meaning of the term, she really makes him present. She not only carries on his work, but she is his very continuation, in a sense far more real than that in which it can be said that any human institution is its founder's continuation.[2]

In his discussion of the sacraments, and especially of the Eucharist, de Lubac showed how "all the sacraments are essentially sacraments of the Church";[3] they are intrinsically social and derive their efficacy from the Church; they in turn build up the Church and make it the sacrament that it is.

On the heels of de Lubac, Karl Rahner developed this type of ecclesiology in several important essays.[4] A second German Jesuit, Otto Semmelroth, wrote a classic exposition of this view in his work, *The Church as Primordial Sacrament.*[5] Since then the idea has been taken up by Schillebeeckx,[6] Smulders,[7] Congar,[8] Groot,[9] Martelet,[10] and many others.

As early as 1949, in a letter concerning the possibility of salvation without actual membership in the Church, the Holy Office said that the Church, like baptism, is a "general aid" to salvation, but it did not go so far as to call the Church explicitly a sacrament.[11] Vatican II, however, took this step in a clear and decisive way. In the first article of its Constitution on the Church, the Council declared that by virtue of its relationship to Christ "the Church is a kind of sacrament of intimate union with God and of the unity of all mankind; that is, she is a sign and instrument of such union and unity." The theme of the Church as basic sacrament recurs in many key passages of Vatican II.[12]

In several Council documents, especially the Constitution on the Liturgy, the sacramental worship of the Church is given a certain primacy over all other forms of Christian life. "The liturgy," we are informed, "is the summit toward which the activity of the Church is directed; at the same time it is the fountain from which all her power flows. For the goal of apostolic works is that all who are made sons of God by faith and baptism should come together to praise God in the midst of His Church, to take part in her sacrifice, and to eat the Lord's Supper."[13] Later in the same Constitution we read that the Church "reveals herself most clearly when a full complement of God's holy people, united in prayer and in a common liturgical service (especially the Eucharist)" actively participate in the official worship of the Church together with their bishop and priests.[14] Thus the Council discerns a connection between the Church as primordial sacrament and the seven ritual sacraments that express, in privileged ways, the sacramentality of the Church as a whole.

The Council, however, does not give a theological explanation of the relationships among Christ, the Church, and the seven ritual sacraments. For such a general theory of sacramentality one would have to turn to philosophical and theological anthropology. In some contemporary philosophical systems, man is seen as a polar unity of spirit and flesh.[15] Man comes to himself by going out of himself. He becomes active only in reception, and receives only through encounter with the world about him. The body mediates that encounter. Without contact with the world through the body, the spirit simply would not actuate itself. As it achieves actuation, it expresses itself in tangible form. Whatever takes place in the recesses of the human spirit somehow comes to visible or tangible expression through the body.

The structure of human life is therefore symbolic. The body with all its movements and gestures becomes the expression of the human spirit. The spirit comes to be what it is in and through the body. The symbolic expression does not simply signify what previously existed independently of it. Rather, the expression and the realization accompany and support each other. The corporeal expression gives the spiritual act the material support it needs in order to achieve itself; and the spiritual act gives shape and meaning to the corporeal expression.

In theological anthropology these philosophical considerations are transposed to the supernatural plane—the plane of man's life in grace whereby he becomes a partaker in the divine nature (2 Pt. 1:4). Man shares in the divine life not in a divine but in a human way, consonantly with his nature as man. The visible and social expression of the life of grace in the Church does not merely signify some spiritual reality that exists prior to its expression, but it sustains the reality of the spiritual activity that it expresses.

Rahner explains this more concretely in his discussion of the sacrament of penance.[16] How does it happen, he asks, that the sacrament can mediate the turning away from sin, if sorrow for sin is necessary for the valid reception of the sacrament? Rahner goes back to the doctrine of the thirteenth-century Scholastics who taught that by virtue of the sacrament itself man's sorrow for sin is intensified and perfected. In the maxim of the schools, "*ex attrito fit contritus, vi clavium.*" In English this may be paraphrased to say: "The experience of sacramental confession and absolution itself transforms the attitude of the sinner so that his initial aversion from sin becomes a sorrow motivated purely by the love of God." Thus the sacrament is both an expression and a source of sorrow. By a kind of mutual priority, the sacrament produces the contrition it expresses, and only by so doing can it become a genuine expression both of man's repentance and of God's powerful mercy toward man.

With this background we may clarify the technical notion of sacrament in theology. A sacrament is, in the first place, a sign of grace. A sign could be a mere pointer to something that is absent, but a sacrament is a "full sign," a sign of something really present. Hence the Council of Trent could rightly describe a sacrament as "the visible form of an invisible grace."[17] Beyond this, a sacrament is an efficacious sign; the sign itself produces or intensifies that of which it is a sign. Thanks to the sign, the reality signified achieves an existential depth; it emerges into solid, tangible existence. Because of the incarnational structure of the human spirit, every reality of the spiritual order necessarily seeks to achieve its proper form of expression, and then lives off the expression it achieves. Thus the Councils can also say that the sacraments contain the grace they signify, and confer the grace they contain.[18] The conferral of a sacrament is an event; it is the self-accomplishment of a grace-filled dynamism seeking an appropriate bodily expression.

As understood in the Christian tradition, sacraments are never merely individual transactions. Nobody baptizes, absolves, or anoints himself, and it is anomalous for the Eucharist to be celebrated in solitude. Here again the order of grace corresponds to the order of nature. Man comes into the world as a member of a family, a race, a people. He comes to maturity through encounter with his fellow men. Sacraments therefore have a dialogic structure. They take place in a mutual interaction that permits the people together to achieve a spiritual breakthrough that they could not achieve in isolation. A sacrament therefore is a socially constituted or communal symbol of the presence of grace coming to fulfillment.

On the basis of this general conception of sacrament we may now turn to two more specific theological notions: those of Christ and of the Church as sacrament.

As Christians we believe that God is good and merciful, that he wills to communicate himself to man in spite of man's sinfulness and resistance to grace. We believe also that God's redemptive will is powerful and efficacious; that it therefore produces effects in history. God's grace is more powerful than man's sinfulness, so that when sin abounded, grace abounded even more (Rom. 5:20). Our belief in the superabundant power of grace when confronted by evil is founded upon the historical tangibility of God's redemptive love in Christ. Jesus Christ is the sacrament of God as turned toward man. He represents for us God's loving acceptance of man and his rehabilitation of man notwithstanding man's unworthiness.

In characterizing Christ as God's sacrament we are looking at Christ as he comes from above. But there is also, so to speak, a "Christology from below."[19] Grace impels men toward communion with God, and as grace works upon men it helps them to express what they are at a given stage in the process of redemption. Only in exteriorizing itself does grace achieve the highest intensity of its realization. Already in the Old Testament, Israel as a people constitutes a sign that historically expresses a real though imperfect yes-saying to God and no-saying to idolatry. Seen from below, Jesus belongs to this tangible history of salvation. As Servant of God he is the supreme sacrament of man's faithful response to God and of God's recognition of that fidelity. The entire history of grace has its summit and crown in Jesus Christ. He is simultaneously the sacrament of God's self-gift and of man's fully obedient acceptance. The mutual acceptance of God and man, initially signified by the history of Israel, reaches its consummation in Christ's cross and resurrection.

Christ, as the sacrament of God, contains the grace that he signifies. Conversely, he signifies and confers the grace he contains. In him the invisible grace of God takes on visible form. But the sacrament of redemption is not complete in Jesus as a single individual. In order to become the kind of sign he must be, he must appear as the sign of God's redemptive love extended toward all mankind, and of the response of all mankind to that redemptive love.

The Church therefore is in the first instance a sign. It must signify in a historically tangible form the redeeming grace of Christ. It signifies that grace as relevantly given to men of every age, race, kind, and condition. Hence the Church must incarnate itself in every human culture.

The Church does not always signify this equally well. It stands under a divine imperative to make itself a convincing sign. It appears most fully as a sign when its members are evidently united to one another and to God through holiness and mutual love, and when they visibly gather to confess their faith in Christ and to celebrate what God has done for them in Christ.

As a sacrament the Church has both an outer and an inner aspect. The institutional or structural aspect of the Church—its external reality—is essential, since without it the Church would not be visible. Visible unity among all Christians is demanded, for without this the sign or communion that the Church is would be fragmented into a multitude of disconnected signs. It is thus of crucial importance that there should be manifest links of continuity among all the particular churches at any given time. Furthermore, it is important that the links should connect the

Church of today with the Church of apostolic times. Otherwise the Church could not appear as the sign of our redemption in and through the historical Christ.

On the other hand, the institutional or structural aspect is never sufficient to constitute the Church. The offices and rituals of the Church must palpably appear as the actual expressions of the faith, hope, and love of living men. Otherwise the Church would be a dead body rather than a living Christian community. It would be an inauthentic sign—a sign of something not really present, and therefore not a sacrament.

But sacrament, as we have been saying, is a sign of grace realizing itself. Sacrament has an event character; it is dynamic. The Church becomes Church insofar as the grace of Christ, operative within it, achieves historical tangibility through the actions of the Church as such.

The Church becomes an actual event of grace when it appears most concretely as a sacrament—that is, in the actions of the Church as such whereby men are bound together in grace by a visible expression. The more widely and intensely the faithful participate in this corporate action of the Church, the more the Church achieves itself.

According to Rahner and others this occurs most fully at the Eucharist:

> Essentially the Church is the historically continuing presence in the world of the incarnate Word of God. She is the historical tangibility of the salvific will of God as revealed in Christ. Therefore the Church is most tangibly and intensively an "event" where (through the words of consecration) Christ himself is present in his own congregation as the crucified and resurrected Saviour, the fount of salvation; where the Redemption makes itself felt in the congregation by becoming sacramentally visible; where the "New and Eternal Testament" which he founded on the cross is most palpably and actu-

ally present in the holy remembrance of its first institution.[20]

The Eucharist is indivisibly Christological and ecclesiological. In its Christological aspect it actualizes in a palpable way the presence of the Redeemer with the congregation of those who look to him in love and trust. In its ecclesiological aspect the Eucharist celebrates and solidifies the union of the faithful with one another about the holy table. Inasmuch as the celebration of the Eucharist is the sacramental anticipation of the heavenly marriage banquet, the final, eternal form of the community of the saints shines forth even now in this solemnity, just as the source of the Church, Christ's own sacrifice, is present in it.

In summary, the Church is not just a sign, but a sacrament. Considered as a bare institution, the Church might be characterized as just an empty sign. It could be going through formalities and be a hollow shell rather than a living community of grace.

But where the Church as sacrament is present, the grace of Christ will not be absent. That grace, seeking its appropriate form of expression—as grace inevitably does—will impel men to prayer, confession, worship, and other acts whereby the Church externally realizes its essence. Through these actions the Church signifies what it contains and contains what it signifies. In coming to expression the grace of the Church realizes itself as grace. The Church therefore confers the grace that it contains, and contains it precisely as conferring it. The Church becomes an event of grace as the lives of its members are transformed in hope, in joy, in self-forgetful love, in peace, in patience, and in all other Christlike virtues.

Does the grace of Christ operate beyond the borders of the visible Church? What could this mean? If the Church is defined as the visible sacrament of Christ's invisible grace, the question may be rephrased to read: Can the grace of Christ be present and operative and yet fail to achieve its appropriate corporate expression? The answer, I suppose, is that the expression is never fully appropriate. The Church never fully achieves itself as Church, at least not in the conditions of this world. It is true Church to the extent that it is tending to become more truly Church. On the other hand, something of the Church as sign will be present wherever the grace of God is effectively at work. The Christological and corporate dimensions of grace will assure a certain ecclesial quality to the life of grace wherever it occurs.

God's gifts are not confined to people who employ biblical or Christian symbolism. The Church understands God as the loving Father of all men; it celebrates and preaches God's redemptive love extended to all. The Church therefore takes it for granted that others besides Christians are recipients of God's grace in Christ.[21] The Church, then, is the place where it appears most clearly that the love that reconciles men to God and to one another is a participation in what God communicates most fully in Christ. Christians are those who see and confess Jesus Christ as the supreme efficacious symbol—the primordial sacrament—of God's saving love stretched out to all.

Wherever the grace of Christ is present, it is in search of a visible form that adequately expresses what it is. In this perspective the Church may be defined as the association of men that palpably bears witness to the true nature and meaning of grace as God's gift in Jesus Christ. Grace disposes a man more and more to receive and profess the gospel of which the Church is the historical bearer. Expressions of grace not historically linked with Christ will be—at least in that respect—more ambiguous.

Before we leave the sacramental model it will be helpful to put to it the three questions already put to the institutional and the communitarian models: What are the bonds of union? Who are the beneficiaries? What is the goal or purpose of the Church?

To the first question one must answer that the bonds are all the social, visible signs of the grace of Christ operative in believing Christians. Grace comes to expression in them when they manifest their faith, hope, and charity by witness, worship, and service. All the Church's doctrinal formularies, liturgies, and pastoral activities have a confessional and doxological dimension. By drawing believers together in witness and worship they reinforce the spiritual unity they express. The witnessing activity of Christians, both in word and in deed, is not seen primarily, as in the institutional model, as a humble compliance with doctrinal laws, nor as a dutiful execution of official directives. Rather it appears as the expression of a heartfelt conviction inspired by the grace of the Holy Spirit. The official magisterium, to be sure, has an indispensable role in helping faith to achieve an appropriate form of expression with an eye to the needs and possibilities of the Church as a whole.

The beneficiaries of the Church, according to this ecclesiology, are all those who are better able to articulate and live their faith thanks to their contact with the believing and loving Church. The sign value of the Church will appear differently to persons differently situated with reference to the community. Since sacramentality by its very nature calls for active participation, only those who belong to the Church, and actively help to constitute it as a sign, share fully in its reality as sacrament. The actions by which they help the Church achieve itself as a visible, social embodiment of God's grace in Christ are means by which their own spiritual life is sustained, intensified, and channeled in constructive ways. To some extent, however, the external spectator, especially if he is expectantly looking out for signs of the presence of the revealing God, may catch some of the significance of the Church as a numinous sign. In the last analysis, no sharp line of demarcation can be drawn between the hesitant member and the sympathetic inquirer. A juridical approach to the question of membership would be out of keeping with the sacramental ecclesiology.

In indicating the beneficiaries of the Church we have already answered, in effect, our third question regarding the benefits. The Church aims to purify and intensify men's response to the grace of Christ. As believers succeed in finding appropriate external forms by which to express their commitment to God in Christ, they become living symbols of divine love and beacons of hope in the world.

From the preceding exposition it should be evident that the sacramental model of the Church has many assets. During the past generation, it has proved highly attractive to professional theologians, at least in the Roman Catholic communion. This model is especially useful in relating the idea of the Church as institution, our first model, with that of the Church as a mystical communion of grace, our second. In this way the sacramental ecclesiology supports the best features of the previous two models while solving problems that prove intractable on either of these other two, such as the relationship between the visible institution and the communion of grace.

A particular advantage of this model is that it can, without neglecting the importance of the visible Church, give ample scope to the workings of divine grace beyond the limits of the institutional Church.

Also pleasing to theologians is the ability of this model to integrate ecclesiology with other traditional theological themes. The doctrine of symbolic, or sacramental, causality brings Christology, ecclesiology, and sacramentology into a single, overarching unity. The inner and outer dimensions of the sacrament, moreover, suggest ways in which the visible means of grace can be successfully related to the doctrine of the Holy Spirit and the spiritual reality of grace.

As a final advantage, we may mention that this model furnishes motives for strong loyalty to the Church and humble striving to adhere to its discipline, while at the same time making room for honest criticism. This ecclesiology does not encourage any deification of the actual form of the Church's life, for it acknowledges that the symbolic expressions of grace are never adequate to the life of grace itself. The Church is continually called to become a better sign of Christ than it has been. In a later chapter, "The True Church," we shall see how the notes of the Church, according to this model, must be conceived in a dynamic and critical way, rather than in the static, apologetic mode that has become associated with the institutional approach.

Some authors have found certain deficiencies in this sacramental type of ecclesiology. One might object that it has comparatively little warrant in Scripture and in the early tradition of the Church, but this objection is certainly not fatal. When Paul speaks of marriage as a mystery or sacrament "in Christ and the Church" (Eph. 5:32) he seems to imply that the Church, like marriage, only more fundamentally, is a sign of loving unity in Christ.

Hamer has given a negative critique of the sacramental definition of the Church, with specific references to Semmelroth and Rahner.[22] In these authors he finds an excessive concern with the external aspects and a corresponding neglect of the inwardness of the mystery of the Church, which he believes to be better safeguarded in his own theory of the Church as communion. It may be questioned whether Hamer does justice to the full thinking of the authors he summarizes, and furthermore whether his critique of these particular authors, even if sustained, would invalidate the sacramental theory of the Church as a whole. In principle, that theory seems to allow for a strong, even a primary, emphasis on the interior and spiritual aspects of the Church.

Another critic, Richard McBrien, observes that in some of the early presentations, such as Schillebeeckx's *Christ the Sacrament of Encounter with God*, there is a narrow sacramentalism that accords insufficient place for *diakonia* (service) in the Church's mission to the world.[23] This is a point we shall have to consider when we come to our fifth model of the Church. In the meantime we may note that this criticism does not impugn the sacramental model of the Church as such. McBrien himself seems to be satisfied with Schillebeeckx's more recent presentations of the Church as "sacrament of dialogue" and "sacrament of the world." Yet it remains true that sacramentalism, carried to excess, can induce an attitude of narcissistic aestheticism that is not easily reconcilable with a full Christian commitment to social and ethical values.

It might also be pointed out that the sacramental ecclesiology is not easily available for preaching. The notion of sacramentality it presupposes is technical and sophisticated, and defies easy popularization. This is not an objection against the theory itself, but it calls attention to a real limitation in the utility of the theory.

Finally, it must be acknowledged that up to the present the sacramental type of ecclesiology has found very little response in Protestant thought. The World Council of Churches at the Uppsala Assembly in 1968 did refer to the Church as "the sign of the coming unity of mankind,"[24] but this seems to be an echo of Vatican Council II rather than a specifically Protestant input. Protestant theology, on the whole, has favored the types of ecclesiology to which we shall turn in our next two chapters.

# V

## The Church as Herald

The model just considered works with the technical term "sacrament," which is understood as a visible or tangible symbolization of grace. This type of ecclesiology emphasizes the present reality of the grace of Christ in the world; the Church is seen as the sign of that reality.

Our next model differs from the preceding because it makes the "word" primary and the "sacrament" secondary. It sees the Church as gathered and formed by the word of God. The mission of the Church is to proclaim that which it has heard, believed, and been commissioned to proclaim. This type of ecclesiology has many points of contact with the communitarian understanding of the Church as People of God, already studied in our third chapter. It differs, however, in that it emphasizes faith and proclamation over interpersonal relations and mystical communion.

This model is kerygmatic, for it looks upon the Church as a herald—one who receives an official message with the commission to pass it on. The basic image is that of the herald of a king who comes to proclaim a royal decree in a public square.

This type of ecclesiology is radically centered upon Jesus Christ and on the Bible as the primary witness to him. It sees the task of the Church primarily in terms of proclamation. In the words of Richard McBrien, who splendidly summarizes the outlook of this ecclesiology:

> This mission of the Church is one of proclamation of the Word of God to the whole world. The Church cannot hold itself responsible for

the failure of men to accept it as God's Word;
it has only to proclaim it with integrity and per-
sistence. All else is secondary. The Church is
essentially a kerygmatic community which holds
aloft, through the preached Word, the wonderful
deeds of God in past history, particularly his
mighty act in Jesus Christ. The community itself
happens wherever the Spirit breathes, wherever
the Word is proclaimed and accepted in faith.
The Church is event, a point of encounter with
God.[1]

The chief proponent of this type of ecclesiology in the
twentieth century is Karl Barth, who draws abundantly on
Paul, Luther, and others. In his *Church Dogmatics* Barth
has a long discussion of the word of God and its relationship to the Church. He warns the Church against so
domesticating the Bible that it would cease to be ruled by
the Bible. The relative distance between the Bible and the
Church, he says, makes it possible for the Bible to testify
against the Church. For the Church to be a place in which
the word of God is truly heard, it is necessary that the
word should never be imprisoned or bracketed by the
Church. The word of God is not a substance immanent in
the Church, but rather an event that takes place as often
as God addresses his people and is believed. The Church
therefore is actually constituted by the word being proclaimed and faithfully heard. The Church is the congregation that is gathered together by the word—a word that
ceaselessly summons it to repentance and reform.[2]

Following in the footsteps of Luther, Barth distinguishes between a theology of glory and a theology of the
cross.[3] The former is found wherever the Church identifies itself with the divine, and points to itself as con-
taining what it proclaims. For Barth this is the prevailing
sin of Catholicism and Modernism. The correct attitude,
according to Barth, is for the Church to point away from
itself like John the Baptist pointing to the Lamb of God.[4]
It calls men to Christ by openly acknowledging its own

emptiness. In the terminology familiar to readers of Barth's *Letter to the Romans*, the Church is the great crater left by the impact of God's revealing word.

The church therefore is not a stable reality that we make an object of our faith. Rather he says:

> We believe the existence of the Church—which means that we believe each particular congregation of Christ. . . . *Credo ecclesiam* means that I believe that here, at this place, in this assembly, the work of the Holy Spirit takes place. By that is not intended a deification of the creature; the Church is not the object of faith, we do not believe *in* the Church; but we do believe that in this congregation the work of the Holy Spirit becomes an event.[5]

In his address to the first Assembly of the World Council of Churches at Amsterdam in 1948, Barth powerfully combined the notions of witness and event:

> In the final period the congregation is the *event* which consists in gathering together (*congregatio*) of those men and women (*fidelium*) whom the living Lord Jesus Christ chooses and calls to be witnesses of the victory He has already won, and heralds of its future manifestation.[6]

Barth's view that the Church is essentially a herald of Christ's Lordship and of the future Kingdom is closely paralleled in Roman Catholic theology by Hans Küng, who began his theological career with a doctoral dissertation on Barth. In his book, *The Church*, Küng has a very characteristic section entitled, "The Eschatological Community of Salvation."[7] He finds that the biblical term *ekklesia* means those summoned by a herald, those who have been called out (*ek-kletoi*).

*Ekklesia,* like "congregation," means both the actual *process of congregating* and the *congregated community* itself: The former should not be overlooked. An *ekklesia* is not something that is formed and founded once and for all and remains unchanged; it becomes an *ekklesia* by the fact of a repeated concrete event, people coming together and congregating, in particular congregating for the purpose of worshipping God. The concrete congregation is the actual manifestation, the representation, indeed the re-alization of the New Testament community.[8]

The local Church, in this theology, is not just a section or province of the Church, as it might appear in some pre-sentations of the institutional model, but is the Church it-self as fully present in each assembly that responds to God's word.[9]

Characteristic of this model, as contrasted with the three previously considered, is a sharp distinction it makes between the Church in its terrestrial form and the King-dom of God, considered as an eschatological reality. Küng stresses that the Church neither is the Kingdom of God, nor does it build the Kingdom, or extend it on earth, or work for its realization. "It is the reign of God which the Church hopes for, bears witness to, proclaims. It is not the bringer or the bearer of the reign of God which is to come and is at the same time already present, but its voice, its announcer, its *herald.* God alone can bring his reign; the Church is devoted entirely to its service."[10]

In Bultmann and the theologians influenced by him one finds an existential variant of kerygmatic theology. In his *Theology of the New Testament,* Bultmann sets forth his views of the relationship between the word of God and the Church, according to St. Paul.[11] He praises Paul for having transferred the eschatological occurrence from the dimension of the cosmos into that of history. Paul, accord-ing to Bultmann, looks upon the eschatological occurrence as something that takes place when the Church actually proclaims Jesus as the crucified and risen Lord. Evangelical preaching is a powerful event in which the hearers are accosted by the personal word of the Sovereign Lord himself, so that the preached word actually becomes the word of God. This word of God, in Bultmann's interpretation of Paul, is constitutive of the Church; it gathers men into a congregation or *ekklesia*.

Speaking for himself, Bultmann in other works insists that the word of God is not a set of timeless ideas but a concrete event, an encounter. Further, the word is eschatological occurrence—that is to say, it makes God present here and now, giving life to those who accept it and death to those who refuse. Human propositions can become the word of God, he says, only in proclamation. In the preaching of the kerygma, the word is authoritative; it becomes event, and the event is Jesus Christ.

> The Word of God and the Church are inseparable. The Church is constituted by the Word of God as the congregation of the elect, and the proclamation of the Word is not a statement of abstract truths, but a proclamation which is duly authorized and therefore needs bearers with proper credentials (2 Cor. 5:18 f.). Just as the Word of God becomes his Word only in event, so the Church is really the Church only when it too becomes an event. For the Church identity with a sociological institution and a phenomenon of the world's history can be asserted only in terms of paradox.[12]

All this sounds very much like Barth, except that Bultmann sees the eschatological occurrence as a present event without necessary ties either to the historical Jesus of the past or to the parousia in the future. This leads to a radical depreciation of the institutional element in the Church, for that element would guarantee historical and geographical continuity. For Bultmann the word validates itself by its present impact on the hearers, since it leads them from fear, anxiety, and inauthenticity to courage, decision, and authenticity.

Bultmann's penetrating analysis of the dynamics of proclamation has left its mark on the so-called post-Bultmannians, Ernst Fuchs and Gerhard Ebeling, who draw on the philosophy of language in Heidegger's later works. For Fuchs it is the recurring "language-event" of proclamation that constitutes the Church:

> Christ means to be understood as the one to whom we belong as *believers*. This happens in the proclamation. But the proclamation does not just bring a conception into language; it decides where Christ, as the one who gathers us, is present, assuming that we give heed to the proclamation and so believe. . . . As the proclamation gathers around Christ, there is no faith without the community of Jesus Christ. And his community has its being, its "togetherness," in the possibility of its being able to speak the kind of language in which the event of its community is fulfilled. This language-*activity* is the mark of the community. *The language of faith brings into language the gathering of faith and thereby Christ.*[13]

For theologians of this school, language has an assembling function. Christian proclamation is therefore to be understood as a linguistic event in which the body of Christ is constituted and assembled. The Church as an assembly takes place in the very activity of proclamation. As James M. Robinson acutely observes, "Here the distinctively Protestant definition of the church in terms of the preaching of the word has been restated in terms of the new hermeneutic's understanding of language."[14]

Our final witness to this kerygmatic ecclesiology, Gerhard Ebeling, stands very close to Fuchs. In his book, *The Nature of Faith*, the chapter on the Church is characteristically entitled "The Summons of Faith." For him the term "summons" fittingly expresses the relationship between the Church and faith; it is more apt than "community," "people," "fellowship," "society," and the like. "You cannot go far wrong, when hearing or speaking of the church, if you remember that it means a summons in matters of faith." The kind of community that the Church is may best be understood by reflecting on the notion of summons:

> . . . the important thing is the togetherness of men who have been reached by the message of faith, who are called and claimed, and form a unity. This unity does not mean a uniform organization. But where the word of faith is heard, the summons becomes acute, there men are gathered together and enter upon a movement which, however different the place and the time and the circumstances, is one movement, since it is a summons in the name of faith. Further, this personal character of the summons is not the whole story. Men do not come together in order to enjoy the fellowship, far less to exhibit themselves as believers. Rather, they are answering a call which surpasses all individual interest, and all community interest based on individuals. There is something more at stake here than is given in the formula, "the community of the faithful." What is at stake is faith itself, and that means what Jesus Christ stands for: the summons to believe, in which each individual is just a serving member.[15]

To grasp more fully the implications of this proclamation model, we may put to it the same questions asked with reference to the models already considered: What are the bonds of union? Who are the beneficiaries? What is the goal or purpose of the Church?

The primary bond of communion in this approach is unquestionably faith; and faith is seen as a response to the gospel, that is to say, the proclamation of the Christ-event. The gospel is understood not as a system of abstract propositional truths, nor as a written document, but rather as the event of proclamation itself. Sacraments in this type of ecclesiology, as contrasted with the institutional and sacramental models, are seen as definitely secondary to the word. For many Protestants in the Reformation tradition the sacrament is understood as a "visible word"—a sign or dramatization of the faith of the community in which they are administered.

The form of Church order in this ecclesiology is characteristically congregational. The Church is regarded as complete in a single local congregation (as the quotations from Küng in this chapter make clear); hence the Church is not dependent for its existence on any worldwide structure. Structural links between local congregations may, however, be desirable to promote mutual interaction and mutual admonition.

The unity of the whole Church will be seen as consisting in the fact that all are responding to one and the same gospel. This theory is open to wide variations in the ways in which local communities of faith structure their creeds, their offices, and their worship. No particular form of church government will be considered essential to the existence of the Church. The tendency is to say that the Church exists wherever there is a community that believes in Christ. "Where two or three are gathered in my name, there am I in the midst of them" (Mt. 18:20). Jesus in the midst of a community gathered in his name: such, according to this ecclesiology, is the very definition of the Church. There can be real unity among congregations insofar as all of them confess Christ and put their trust in him.

The beneficiaries of the Church, according to this type of ecclesiology, are those who hear the word of God and put their faith in Jesus as Lord and Savior. Faith, understood in the sense of a reliant commitment to Jesus Christ, is regarded as the necessary condition for receiving the salvation that God promises in Jesus Christ.

The goal of the Church, in this style of theology, is simply to herald the message. This ecclesiology goes with a strong evangelistic missionary thrust. The Church's responsibility is not necessarily to produce conversion (only God can do that), still less to build the Kingdom of God; but rather to evangelize all the nations in accordance with the "great commission" of Mt. 28:18–20.

The preaching of the gospel is related to salvation, because it summons men to put their faith in Jesus as Savior. It announces the day of salvation that is at hand for believers. More than this, the preaching is itself an eschatological event. The word of God, on the lips of the authorized herald, is impregnated with the power of God himself, whose word it becomes. The word saves those who believe in it. Conversely, it condemns those who refuse to believe. The preaching of the Church, as it resounds in all corners of the earth, ushers in the saving presence of God. The word carries with it in promise the reality of the salvation to which it bears witness. For Bultmann and his disciples, one may say that the acceptance of the gospel actually *is* salvation. The authoritative heralding of the story of the cross and resurrection brings authentic existence to those who respond in faith.

What are the strengths and weaknesses of this fourth model? On the credit side of the ledger one will have to list many important points. For one thing, it has a good biblical foundation in the prophetic tradition of the Old Testament, in Paul, and elsewhere. Secondly, this ecclesiology gives a clear sense of identity and mission to the Church—especially the local church—as a congregation that heralds the good news of Jesus Christ and sets its face against all idolatry. Thirdly, it is conducive to a spirituality that focuses on God's sovereignty and on man's infinite distance from him. This ecclesiology leads to obedience, humility, and readiness for repentance and reform. Finally, this theory, as propounded by Barth and the dialectical school, gives rise to a very rich theology of the word. The word is rightly seen as far more than a representation of ideas, more than a source of information, more than an explanation of what is antecedently real, but as expression of the person, as address, as a bond of communion between persons in dialogue. As contrasted with the image or the sacrament, the word has a unique capacity to express not only what is present but what is absent, not only what is but also what is not, and hence to protest against what is actually given and to condemn it. All these points, well developed in the Protestant theology of the word, are valuable correctives to the Catholic tendency to focus on complacency, on celebration, on sacramentality.

Yet there are limitations to this ecclesiological type, and the Catholic theological tradition is especially well equipped to voice a word of criticism. The Catholic point of view (and here the term "catholic" should perhaps be spelled with a lower-case "c" because many non-Romans will join in the critique) stresses the incarnational aspect of the Christian revelation. It is not enough to speak of the word of God, for Christianity stands or falls with the affirmation that the Word has been made flesh. In the theology of proclamation, on the lips of some Protestants, it appears as though the Word has become not flesh but only word! Here the reader would do well to recall de Lubac's remarks about how Christ perpetuates not only his doctrine and his work in the Church, but shares with it his very being.[16]

Bishop Lesslie Newbigin, of the Church of South India, has objected that on Barth's view the Church seems to dissolve into a series of totally disconnected happenings. The Bible, he says, regards the Church as a divine-human fellowship realized in a real, visible community existing continuously in world history.[17] For such a community to perdure, there is need of a continuing institution. The institutional should not simply be played off against either the event or the community.

> Is it not significant that the deepest, most fruitful, and most satisfying personal relationships are those in which the impersonal factors are at their maximum, in which the person

is most indissolubly connected with the physical, biological, and economic factors—namely in marriage and the family? And must we not assert that the attempt to isolate the personal, and to set it over against the legal and institutional, does violence to its nature? Must one not say that the attempt, in the conditions of human nature, to have a personal relation divorced from its proper impersonal context is futile? It is surely congruous with the whole nature of man that Christ, in giving us Himself, has given us a Church which is His body on earth and therefore marked by visible limits and a continuing structure, so that fellowship with Him should be incorporation in it.[18]

Vatican II attempted to capitalize on various themes derived from the Barthian theology of the word, but it was not satisfied with a merely prophetic understanding of the word. In the Constitution on the Liturgy, for instance, we read that Christ "is present in His word, since it is He Himself who speaks when the holy Scriptures are read in the church. He is present, finally, when the Church prays and sings, for He promised: 'When two or three are gathered together for my sake, there am I in the midst of them' (Mt. 18:20)."[19] But in the same paragraph the Council spoke of Christ's presence in the sacraments, and especially in the Eucharist.

The Constitution on Divine Revelation begins on a markedly kerygmatic note, with the phrase "hearing the word of God with reverence and proclaiming it confidently," but it immediately goes on to quote from the first letter of John, "We announce to you the eternal life which was with the Father, and has appeared to us. What we have seen and have heard we announce to you, in order that you may have fellowship with us. . . ."[20] Thus the word mediates not only what was heard but what appeared and was seen, and the goal of preaching is not mere profession of faith in the message, but rather a communion of life and love.

The Catholic understanding of the Church as a stable community in history, in which Christ continues to make himself present and available, leads to a different view of authority in the Church. The magisterium of the Church is, to be sure, not over the word of God but under it,[21] but the living magisterium is seen to be endowed with authority from Christ to interpret the word for the community. This affects the understanding of the relationship between the Scriptures and the Church. Whereas in some Protestant traditions the magisterium is seen as subject to correction by private scholarship, Catholicism tends to emphasize the subjection of scholars to the official teaching office. As noted in the Decree on Ecumenism,

> But when Christians separated from us affirm the divine authority of the sacred Books, they think differently from us—different ones in different ways—about the relationship between the Scriptures and the Church. In the Church, according to Catholic belief, an authentic teaching office plays a special role in the explanation and proclamation of the written word of God.[22]

A final criticism that is voiced by Catholics—and not by Catholics alone—with regard to this type of ecclesiology is that it focuses too exclusively on witness to the neglect of action. It is too pessimistic or quietistic with regard to the possibilities of human effort to establish a better human society in this life, and the duty of Christians to take part in this common effort. Typical of this school is the reaction of Karl Barth to the Vatican II Constitution on the Church in the Modern World. He asks two questions:

> 1. Does the thorough optimism of this Constitution over the possibilities of the development of the world correspond to the emphases of the Synoptic Gospels and the Letters of Paul?

2. Is it so certain that dialogue with the world is to be placed ahead of proclamation to the world?[23]

Many contemporary Christians inside and outside Roman Catholicism feel, contrary to Barth, that the secular theology of Vatican II was a major step forward. McBrien speaks for this constituency when he criticizes Küng's conception of the Kingdom of God:

> . . . his basic understanding of the Kingdom seems too much dominated by the Lutheran influence. The Kingdom is totally a work of God, produced entirely and exclusively at his initiative. The posture of man is one of humble acceptance and patient expectation. . . .
>
> In this laudable concern to break the Gordian knot between the Church and the Kingdom of God, Küng seems to me to have overemphasized the discontinuity and to have adopted a strongly Lutheran understanding of the Church as a community of proclamation rather than of sociopolitical *diakonia*.[24]

In broaching this criticism, we are already beginning to anticipate still another ecclesiological type: that of the Church as an agent for the betterment of the human community in the world at large. This theme will be the subject of our following chapter.

# VI

# The Church as Servant

All the models thus far considered give a primary or privileged position to the Church with respect to the world. In the institutional models, the official Church teaches, sanctifies, and rules with the authority of Christ. In the communion models, the Church is viewed as God's People or Christ's Body, growing into the final perfection of the Kingdom. In the sacramental ecclesiologies, the Church is understood as the visible manifestation of the grace of Christ in human community. Finally, in the herald models, the Church takes on an authoritarian role, proclaiming the gospel as a divine message to which the world must humbly listen.

In all these models the Church is seen as the active subject, and the world as the object that the Church acts upon or influences. The Church is produced by God's direct action, and stands as a kind of mediator between God and the world. God comes to the world through the Church, and the world likewise comes to God through the Church—insofar as men believe the Church, join it, and obey its teachings.

Since the dawn of modern times, and especially since the Enlightenment, the world has become increasingly active and independent of the Church. The various sciences and disciplines have one by one emancipated themselves from Church control, and generally benefited from their emancipation. In the secularized world of our time, the arts and sciences, industry and government go on developing their own forms according to their own inner logic. The Church admonishes the world, but the world, generally speaking, feels justified in paying no heed. It devises its own techniques and methods, expecting no help from Church authority.

Especially since the middle of the nineteenth century, the Church has missed no opportunity to point out that the world was falling into serious difficulties by seeking to develop without regard to Church regulations. The papal encyclicals from Gregory XVI (1831–46) to Pius XII (1939–58) continually deplore modern errors. The *Syllabus of Errors*, published by Pius IX in 1864, comes to a climax with Error No. 80: "The Roman pontiff can and should reconcile himself with, and adjust to, progress, liberalism, and recent civilization."[1] In 1907 the Church condemned Modernism, a movement that had begun as an effort by Catholics to bring the Church abreast of the times. Much later, just as World War II was breaking out, Pius XII issued his first encyclical, *Darkness over the Earth* (*Summi Pontificatus*, Oct. 20, 1939), reflecting remnants of this antimodernist mentality:

> As you know, Worshipful Brethren, the reason why the principles of morality in general have been so long set aside in Europe is the defection of so many minds from Christian doctrine, of which Blessed Peter's See is the appointed guardian and teacher. . . .
> They did not guess what would follow, when the truth which sets us free had been exchanged for the lie that makes slaves of us. In repudiating God's law, so fatherly, so infinitely wise, and Christ's commandments, breathing of charity, uniting men together and drawing their minds to things above, they did not reflect that it would mean handing themselves over to a capricious ruler, the feeble and grovelling wisdom of man. They boasted of progress, when they were in fact relapsing into decadence; they conceived that they were reaching heights of achievement when they were miserably forfeiting their human dignity; they claimed that this century of ours

was bringing maturity and completion with it, when they were being reduced to a pitiable form of slavery.[2]

Pope John XXIII, and Vatican Council II, which he so largely inspired, register a dramatic change of attitude. The apostolic constitution convoking Vatican II reads almost as though it were a rebuttal of Pius XII's *Darkness over the Earth*. Pope John declares: "Distrustful souls see only darkness burdening the face of the earth. We, instead, like to reaffirm all our confidence in our Savior, who has not left the world he redeemed."[3] The new council, he predicted, would be "a demonstration of the Church, always living and always young, which feels the rhythm of the times and which in every century beautifies itself with new splendor, radiates new light, achieves new conquests. . . ."[4]

In his opening address at the first session in 1962, Pope John returned to the same themes. He firmly dissociated himself from those who "in these modern times . . . can see nothing but prevarication and ruin."[5]

The Pastoral Constitution on the Church in the Modern World, the most novel and distinctive contribution of Vatican II, outlines a completely new understanding of the relationship between the Church and the world of our day. It recognizes the "legitimate autonomy" of human culture and especially of the sciences;[6] it calls upon the Church to update itself—including its doctrine and institutional structures[7]—so as to appropriate the best achievements of modern secular life. It affirms that the Church must respect the accomplishments of the world and learn from them, lest it fall behind the times and become incapable of effectively heralding the gospel.[8] Finally, it asserts that the Church should consider itself as part of the total human family, sharing the same concerns as the rest of men. Thus in Article 3, after asserting that the Church should enter into conversation with all men, the Constitution teaches that just as Christ came into the world not to be served but to serve, so the Church, carrying on the mission of Christ, seeks to serve the world by fostering the brotherhood of all men. The same theme is recapitulated in the conclusion, Article 92.

The theological method accompanying this type of ecclesiology differs from the more authoritarian types of theology that have become familiar to us in past centuries. This method may be called "secular-dialogic": secular, because the Church takes the world as a properly theological locus, and seeks to discern the signs of the times; dialogic, because it seeks to operate on the frontier between the contemporary world and the Christian tradition (including the Bible), rather than simply apply the latter as a measure of the former.[9]

The image of the Church that best harmonizes with this attitude is that of Servant. The servant theme, already intimated in the Vatican II documents, has been taken up more strongly since the Council. A notable example is the pastoral letter, "The Servant Church," issued by Cardinal Cushing of Boston in Advent 1966. In its opening section this letter sets forth powerfully the image of Christ the Servant:

> Jesus came not only to proclaim the coming of the Kingdom, he came also to give himself for its realization. He came to serve, to heal, to reconcile, to bind up wounds. Jesus, we may say, is in an exceptional way the Good Samaritan. He is the one who comes alongside of us in our need and in our sorrow, he extends himself for our sake. He truly dies that we might live and he ministers to us that we might be healed.[10]

Then in a second section the pastoral argues that the Church must be the body of Christ, the suffering servant, and hence the servant Church. "So it is that the Church announces the coming of the Kingdom not only in word, through preaching and proclamation, but more particularly in work, in her ministry of reconciliation, of binding up wounds, of suffering service, of healing. . . . And the

Lord was the 'man for others,' so must the Church be 'the community for others.' "[11]

Then the pastoral letter goes on to apply this doctrine to the individual Christian, who is called to be a "man for others" standing at the side of Jesus in the service of the neighbor. In later sections the pastoral goes on to apply this to certain specific apostolates: the pursuit of peace, the alleviation of poverty, the elimination of racism, and the reconciliation of churches.

A similar servant ecclesiology underlies many other official Church statements since 1966. Remarkable in this respect are the Presbyterian Confession of 1967, the Uppsala Report of the World Council of Churches in 1968, the Conclusions of the Second General Conference of Latin American Bishops at Medellin in 1968, and the document on Justice in the World issued by the Roman Catholic Synod of Bishops at its fall meeting in 1971.

For the most part, however, the official statements of the churches simply register and sanction ideas that have been previously developed by theologians. The new secular thrust in ecclesiology was prepared by the thought of a number of twentieth-century theologians, two of whom may be selected for special mention: Teilhard de Chardin and Dietrich Bonhoeffer.

Teilhard wrestled all his life to achieve a reconciliation between his two great loyalties—the one toward science and the other toward the Church. His double vocation as anthropologist and as priest made him feel that he must not be pulled apart. There must be an ultimate unity, he felt, between theology and science, between religion and technology, between the Church and the world. His synthesis was Christocentric. He maintained that all the energies in the universe were ultimately converging on Christ, and hence on the Church as the "consciously Christified portion of the world." The Church, he held, is the main focal point of the energies of love in the world; it is the "central axis of universal convergence and the exact meeting point that emerges between the universe and the Omega point."[12] According to Teilhard, the Church is necessary to prevent the vital energies of the world from becoming uselessly dissipated. On the other hand, the world is necessary to the Church, lest the Church should "wither like a flower out of water."[13] In substance, then, Teilhard taught that the Church is divinely called to be a progressive society, the spearhead of the axis of evolution, and that, in order to fulfill this vocation, it must be open to everything good that emerges from the dynamism of the human spirit as found in science and technology. His view is still moderately ecclesiocentric, but he finds evidences of a thrust toward Omega in the movement of the world even beyond the borders of the Church.

As regards Dietrich Bonhoeffer, we have already seen that in his early works, especially *The Communion of Saints,* he places a heavy emphasis on the nature of the Church as a communion of men drawn together by Christ. Subsequently, in his *Ethics,* he moves toward a more kerygmatic position, corresponding to our fourth type of ecclesiology. "The intention of the preacher," he writes, "is not to improve the world, but to summon it to belief in Jesus Christ and to bear witness to the reconciliation which has been accomplished through Him and His dominion."[14]

Finally, in his posthumously published *Letters and Papers from Prison,* Bonhoeffer becomes quite critical of Barth's kerygmatic theology, characterizing it as revelational positivism. He calls for a humble and servant Church:

> The Church is the Church only when it exists for others. To make a start, it should give away all its property to those in need. The clergy must live solely on the free-will offerings of their congregations, or possibly engage in some secular calling. The Church must share in the secular problems of ordinary human life, not dominating, but helping and serving.[15]

Both Teilhard and Bonhoeffer were obsessed with the

feeling that the world was passing the Church by, while the Church proudly assumed that it already had all the answers to the world's problems from revelation. They tried to get the Church to take seriously the secular achievements of modern man, and they sought to ground their positive attitude toward the world theologically and Christologically. For Teilhard, Christ was the Omega, the spearhead of the axis of evolution. For Bonhoeffer, Christ was the "beyond in the midst," and, in his universal lordship, Lord even of those who had no religion. In his humanity, according to Bonhoeffer, Christ appears as the man without selfishness and without defenses, the man for others. In order to be a credible witness to him, the Church must adopt his style of life.

Since the early sixties, nearly all the ecclesiologists who have emerged into prominence have been representative of this new style of secular-dialogic theology. In English-speaking Protestantism and Anglicanism, the best-known representatives of this ecclesiology are Gibson Winter, Harvey Cox, and John A. T. Robinson. Gibson Winter, in his *The New Creation as Metropolis*, calls for a "servant Church"—one that is "no longer an institutional structure of salvation alongside the worldly structures of restraint" but one that is "that community within the worldly structures of historical responsibility which recognizes and acknowledges God's gracious work for all mankind. The servant Church is the community who confirm mankind in its freedom to fashion its future, protesting the pretensions to ultimacy in any human structures and suffering with men in the struggle against the powers of evil."[16] He proposes that the apostolate of the servant Church should not be primarily one of confessional proclamation or of cultic celebration, but rather discerning reflection on God's promise and presence in the midst of our own history.[17]

Harvey Cox, building on the work of Gibson Winter and others, included in his *The Secular City* a characteristic chapter, "The Church as God's Avant-garde." "The church's task in the secular city," he wrote, "is to be the *diakonos* of the city, the servant who bends himself to struggle for its wholeness and health."[18]

Following up on Harvey Cox and upon his own previous work on the notion of the Kingdom of God, the Anglican bishop John A. T. Robinson, in *The New Reformation?*, argued that the Church is in drastic need of a stripping down of its structures, which can be an obstacle to its mission. To be of service the Church must work within the structures of the world rather than build parallel structures. "The house of God is not the Church but the world. The Church is the servant, and the first characteristic of a servant is that he lives in someone else's house, not his own."[19]

A parallel development, not uninfluenced by the authors just mentioned, has been under way in Roman Catholic ecclesiology since the Council. Robert Adolfs in *The Grave of God* uses as his key concept the Pauline notion of *kenosis*. Jesus "emptied himself (*hēauton ekenosen*)," says Paul in Philippians 2:7, "taking the form of a servant." For Adolfs this means that Jesus divested himself of all craving for power and dignity. The Church, if it is to be like Christ, must similarly renounce all claims to power, honors, and the like; it must not rule by power but attract by love.[20] Eugene Bianchi, in his *Reconciliation: The Function of the Church*, maintains that the most fundamental mission of the Church is that of reconciliation, the overcoming of the various alienations that vex humanity today. This calls for "a humble and servant approach to the world already touched by redemption."[21]

Another American Roman Catholic, Richard P. McBrien, has strongly developed the theme of the servant Church. He wrote his doctoral dissertation on John Robinson, whose thought he reflects and develops. McBrien makes it quite clear that the Church must not look upon itself as "a humanitarian social agency, or a group of like-minded individuals sharing a common perspective and moving here and there, wherever 'the action is.' If the theological reality of the Church goes no deeper than that, there seems little reason to perpetuate this community in history or to continue one's personal affiliation with it."[22] The Church for McBrien is the universal sacrament of salvation and the Body of Christ; but just because it is all this, it has a mandate to serve. "The Church must offer itself as one of the principal agents whereby the human community is made to stand under the judgment of the enduring values of the Gospel of Jesus Christ: freedom, justice, peace, charity, compassion, reconciliation."[23]

With this sampling of contemporary servant ecclesiologics we may now ask of this model our usual three questions: What are the bonds of union? Who are the beneficiaries? What is the goal or purpose of the Church? The bonds of union, according to secular ecclesiologists, are not so much the traditional bonds of doctrine and sacramental communion, but rather the sense of mutual brotherhood that springs up among those who join in Christian service toward the world. As will be seen in Chapter IX, some assert that these bonds cut right through the traditional denominational divisions and forge a new communion among those who had been ecclesiastically estranged from one another.

The beneficiaries of the Church's action, in this type of ecclesiology, are not exclusively, or even primarily, the members of the Church itself. Rather they are all those brothers and sisters the world over, who hear from the Church a word of comfort or encouragement, or who obtain from the Church a respectful hearing, or who receive from it some material help in their hour of need.

The Church's mission, in the perspectives of this theology, is not primarily to gain new recruits for its own ranks, but rather to be of help to all men, wherever they are. The special competence of the Church is to keep alive the hope and aspiration of men for the Kingdom of God and its values. In the light of this hope the Church is able to discern the signs of the times and to offer guidance and prophetic criticism. In this way the Church promotes the mutual reconciliation of men and initiates them in various ways into the Kingdom of God.

Like other models of the Church, this servant ecclesiology has both strengths and weaknesses. Its strongest claim to acceptance lies in the new situation in which the Church presently finds itself. Too much turned in upon itself, the Church has become increasingly concerned with its own internal affairs and correspondingly more estranged from modern civilization, to the point where communication between the Church and the world has become very difficult. This has brought about in the Church a loss of numbers, a loss of vitality, and a loss of influence. The language and structures of the Church have not kept pace with the development of human culture in general.

On the other hand, it may be convincingly argued that the modern world very much needs something the Church alone can give: faith in Christ, hope in the ultimate coming of God's kingdom, and commitment to the values of peace, justice, and human brotherhood, all of which are dominant biblical themes. While all men can perhaps see the desirability of values such as these, they feel helpless in making these values prevail. Individuals and groups become sucked into a cynical quest for power and success. The Christian faith can motivate men, as perhaps nothing else can, to employ their power for service.

The servant ecclesiology reflects a consciousness of these needs of both the Church and the world. It seeks to give the Church a new relevance, a new vitality, a new modernity, and a new sense of mission. The effort on the Church's part to overcome its pride, its corporate egoism, and its callousness toward human misery promises to bring about a great spiritual renewal within the Church itself. Not only individual persons in the Church, but the Church itself, can be transformed into altruistic service toward the poor and the oppressed. This service can include prophetic criticism of social institutions, and thus help to transform human society into the image of the promised Kingdom.

One serious objection to this theory is its lack of any direct biblical foundation. While service is often extolled, the Bible does not seem to envision the task of the Church as service. In the parables Jesus evidently places high value on material and spiritual help to one's fellow men in need, and there is no reason to think that this demand does not weigh upon the Church as a whole. In speaking of the community of his disciples as light of the world and salt of the earth, Jesus clearly has in mind some kind of beneficial influence. But this could be interpreted primarily in terms of the ministry of word and sacrament, in accordance with the previous models of the Church, rather than in terms of caritative service.

The term "servant," indeed, contains certain ambiguities. It connotes three things: work done not freely but under orders; work directed to the good of others rather than to the worker's own advantage; and work that is humble and demeaning ("servile").

In the first of these senses, neither Christ nor the Christian is supposed to be the world's servant. Jesus is obedient, not to the world but to the Father. He is the servant of God, not of men, and we too are called to be servants of God. Paradoxically, the service of God, according to the New Testament, leads to the freedom of sonship, whereas the refusal to serve God leads to the captivity of sin.

In the second sense, the term "servant" can be and is applied to Christ or the Christian. He works out of love, and hence for the true good of the other. In the third sense, too, service becomes the Christian. Like Jesus, we are called to wash one another's feet.

The term *diakonia* is certainly one of the most important New Testament terms applied to the Church.[24] The term applies to all types of ministry—including the ministry of the word, of sacraments, and of temporal help. All offices in the Church are forms of *diakonia*, and thus the term, in biblical usage, cannot properly be used in opposition to preaching or worship. Furthermore, the *diakonia* that goes on in the Church is generally if not always seen as the behavior of Christians toward one another. It would be surprising to find in the Bible any statement that the Church as such is called upon to perform *diakonia* toward the world. It would not have entered the mind of any New Testament writer to imagine that the Church has a mandate to transform the existing social institutions, such as slavery, war, or the Roman rule over Palestine.

The modern notion of the "servant Church" therefore seems to lack any direct foundation in the Bible. Yet it may not be out of place to speak of an "indirect foundation." The so-called Servant Songs in Isaiah are applicable to the Church as well as to Christ. Of the Servant it is said, "I have given you as a covenant to the people, a light to the nations, to open the eyes that are blind, to bring out the prisoners from the dungeon, from the prison those who sit in darkness" (Is. 42:6–7). And the Servant describes his mission in words that Jesus himself would quote: "The Spirit of the Lord God is upon me, because the Lord has anointed me to bring good tidings to the afflicted; he has sent me to bind up the brokenhearted, to proclaim liberty to the captives, and the opening of the prison to those who are bound . . ." (Is. 61:1; cf. Lk. 4:16–19).

Closely connected with the question of the "servant Church" is the problem of how the Church is related to the Kingdom of God. Robinson, McBrien, and others would say that the Church is not the Kingdom, but is merely one of a number of agencies within history that are building up the future Kingdom of God. The servant role of the Church consists in its dedication to the transformation of the world into the Kingdom. As already mentioned, McBrien and Küng differ in their understanding of this point.[25] Küng would seem to have the better exegetes on his side when he contends that the Kingdom of God is viewed in the New Testament as God's work, not man's. Still less does the New Testament envisage other agencies than the Church as heralds or catalysts of God's Kingdom. Scripture scholars such as Gerald O'Collins say that they cannot find anywhere in the New Testament the idea that there are people called to the Kingdom without also being called to the Church.[26] This seems to be a modern development, and if it can be justified at all, the justification will have to be on grounds other than biblical.

For the contemporary reader it is surprising to see how

little the New Testament makes of the Church's responsibility toward the temporal order. In the Old Testament the Kingdom is seen as a reign of peace and justice among men, with an abundance of material blessings for all. In the name of the Kingdom—or, preferably, kingship—of God, the prophets condemn rulers who are violent and oppressive. On this analogy one might be able to work out a biblical argument in favor of a sociopolitical role for the Church. But the argument could only be indirect, for in the New Testament, where the notion of the Church is explicitly addressed, salvation is individualized and spiritualized. The emphasis is apocalyptic rather than prophetic. The Church is seen as existing for the glory of God and of Christ, and for the salvation of its members in a life beyond the grave. It is not suggested that it is the Church's task to make the world a better place to live in.

The same supernaturalistic individualism that we have observed in the New Testament may be found in much of the theological tradition. Congar has pointed out the common tendency to apply the evangelical directives regarding humility and sacrifice only to individuals rather than to the Church as such. "Is it the individual alone," he asks, "who must be the servant and not the master, who must forgive offenses, bless his enemies and not curse them? Have themes such as these any longer a place in an ecclesiology identified in practice with a treatise on public ecclesiastical law?"[27]

As the institutional model of the Church recedes from its primacy, there is a shift from the categories of power to the categories of love and service. We may welcome the current stress on the servant Church as a sign of spiritual progress. But the concept of service must be carefully nuanced so as to keep alive the distinctive mission and identity of the Church.

Some radical proponents of the secular ecclesiology so emphasize the importance of peace, justice, and prosperity in this life that they lead one to question whether there is any authentic hope for persons to whom these goals are unattainable. One wonders whether the Church would have a message of comfort for someone who, through no fault of his own, was dying poor and friendless. Traditionally, Christianity has always appeared as good news, especially for the hungry, the wretched, and the persecuted—those who, humanly speaking, have no right to hope at all. According to the Sermon on the Mount, the Kingdom belongs especially to those who are poor and persecuted in this life.

Interpreted in the light of the gospel, the Kingdom of God cannot be properly identified with abstract values such as peace, justice, reconciliation, and affluence. The New Testament personalizes the Kingdom. It identifies the Kingdom of God with the gospel, and both of them with Jesus. As Paul says in 1 Cor. 1:30, God has made Jesus himself our wisdom, our justice, our sanctification, and our redemption. Not to know Jesus and not to put one's faith in him is therefore a serious failure. It is not to know the Kingdom as it really should be known. The Christian believes that anyone who is committed to the Kingdom of God is in some sense, at least implicitly, committed to Jesus Christ. Acknowledging Jesus as Lord of all, the Christian wishes, so far as possible, to make Jesus known to all men. The notion of the Kingdom of God, which is rightly used by secular theologians to point up the dimension of social responsibility, should not be separated from the preaching of Jesus as Lord. The servant notion of the Kingdom, therefore, goes astray if it seeks to set itself up in opposition to the kerygmatic.

# VII

# The Church and Eschatology

Today we commonly think of the Church as a this-worldly entity. It is often said that at the end of time the Church will cease to be. In the words of Rahner, the Church "is living always on the proclamation of her own provisional status and of her historically advancing elimination in the coming kingdom of God towards which she is expectantly travelling as a pilgrim."[1] The Church, according to McBrien, exists not for its own sake but for the sake of the Kingdom.[2] Hans Küng, in an eloquent passage, asserts that the Church is essentially something of the present, something finite, whereas the Kingdom of God belongs to the future, to the end-time. *Ecclesia*, says Küng, is the work of man; but *basileia*, he maintains, is the work of God.[3] Pannenberg likewise maintains that "Christ points the Church toward the Kingdom of God that is beyond the Church"—a thesis he attempts to establish with the help of some biblical references.[4]

To set oneself against all these authorities is to be very bold, and yet that is exactly what I propose to do.[5] I cannot agree that the Church is a temporary, this-worldly reality, still less that—as Küng would have it—it is definitively the work of man. As I see it, the modern practice of contrasting the Church and the Kingdom as these authors do tends to obscure and distort the biblical conceptions of both Church and Kingdom.

At the outset it seems worthwhile to note that the term *ekklesia* as used in the New Testament is an eschatological term. It means an assembly or convocation and more specifically the convocation of the saints that will be realized to the full at the eschaton. In a recent study the

Swedish exegete Harald Riesenfeld has shown how the idea of "the people of the saints of the Most High," upon whom, according to Dan. 7:27, power and glory are to be bestowed, lies at the root of the thinking of Paul, the Synoptics, and presumably even Jesus concerning the Church.[6] Thus Paul can say in 1 Cor. 6:1–3 that the Christians, as saints, are chosen to have a share in God's power of judgment, even over the angels. In Col. 1:12–13 he affirms that already here on earth God has transferred us into the Kingdom of his beloved Son and has qualified us to share in the inheritance of the saints in light.

On the basis of nearly all the images of the Church in Scripture, one is led to believe that the Church, far from passing away at the end of time, will then truly come into its own. In the preaching of Jesus, the Church is the little flock who are being led into the heavenly pastures. The eschatological meals that Jesus celebrates with his disciples are a foretaste of the final messianic supper in the Kingdom of heaven. Jesus goes before his disciples to prepare a place for them in his Father's house. Nothing suggests that the community of the disciples will be dissolved in heaven, when the twelve sit on thrones judging the twelve tribes of Israel.

In the Pauline letters, the Church is the Temple that will be completed and consecrated at the end of history. It is also the Body of Christ, still growing up into him who is the head, Jesus Christ (Eph. 4:15). The letter to the Hebrews depicts the Christian community as a covenant people living in exile and hastening to the Sabbath rest. The Johannine Apocalypse likewise gives an eschatological vision of the Church. It closes with a climactic vision of the final consummation, in which the glorious Church is depicted under the images of the holy city, the new Jerusalem coming down out of heaven from God, and the bride adorned for her husband. The company of the saints, which proclaims with one voice the glory of God and of the Lamb, is the Church in its true and finished form.

Throughout the Patristic and medieval periods, theologians constantly spoke of two forms of the Church: an imperfect earthly form in which the Church was still struggling to achieve its true reality, and a perfect, heavenly form in which the Church enjoyed the blessed vision of God. In the later Middle Ages this distinction was hardened into something approaching a division. The *ecclesia militans* was frequently contrasted with the *ecclesia triumphans,* but the term *ecclesia* was considered to apply more perfectly to the latter than to the former. For reasons soon to be discussed, the idea of the heavenly or triumphant Church has receded into the background since the High Middle Ages, and in modern times the term "Church" has been almost exclusively identified with what medieval theologians would have called the "pilgrim" or "militant" Church. In Vatican II, however, we note a happy change of emphasis. *Lumen gentium* devotes an entire chapter to the theme, "The Eschatological Nature of the Pilgrim Church and Her Union with the Heavenly Church." This chapter directly declares that the Church will attain its full perfection only in the glory of heaven.[7]

To discuss the relationship between the Church and the eschaton in twentieth-century theology is no simple task, because each of the terms, Church and eschaton, can be understood in a number of different ways. There are at least as many eschatologies in currency as there are ecclesiologies. Richard McBrien categorizes these into the following five basic types:[8]

(1) Consistent, consequent, futurist, or thoroughgoing eschatology;

(2) Realized eschatology;

(3) Existentialist eschatology;

(4) Salvation-history eschatology, and

(5) Proleptic eschatology.

In combination with the five ecclesiologies we have listed, this would yield a total of twenty-five possible relationships between the terms "Church" and "eschaton"— too many to analyze in a single chapter. But fortunately it will not be necessary to treat every one of these logical possibilities.

The first and second of McBrien's five eschatologies represent extreme positions: the purely futurist and the purely realized options. The first of these positions is very rare, or perhaps not really possible, in Christian theology. Christianity, after all, is founded on the conviction that Jesus is the Christ, and that he by his life, death, and resurrection has accomplished what was necessary for the redemption of man. Holding that Jesus is the Messiah or the last Adam, Christians are distinguished from Jews by their view that the messianic age is already upon us. The Spirit of Christ, the messianic gift, has already been poured forth on Pentecost.

What then is meant by "consistent" or "consequent" eschatology—the position commonly associated with the names of Johannes Weiss, Albert Schweitzer, and Martin Werner? According to these scholars, Jesus believed that God's eschatological Kingdom was about to come; he looked forward to it as something future, and did not claim to embody it in his own person. In their basic contentions these authors were probably on good exegetical grounds—for, after all, Jesus did preach before the first Easter. At least a number of reported sayings of Jesus seem to indicate that he did hold a futurist view of the Kingdom. Some of these scholars—Werner in particular—argue that even after the death of Jesus the Christian community for some years held that the messianic age lay in the very near future, and only when it did not arrive did they shift to a kind of "realized eschatology" that has become characteristic of the Church since the first century. This again is a historical question, and the answer to it tells us nothing about the doctrinal question whether Christians today are to look forward to the kind of parousia that was expected, allegedly, by Jesus and the Christians of the first generation.

To be accurate, most of the theologians of the "consistent eschatology" school are not personally committed to any such futurism. Weiss rejected the other-worldly fanaticism of Jesus, as he regarded it, with the statement that, having one foot already in the next world, Jesus could have nothing in common with us who live in this world.[9]

Schweitzer argued that Jesus hoped by his death to bring in the eschaton, but failed. Instead he was crushed by the wheel of history. The experience of nearly two millennia of the delayed parousia, Schweitzer added, makes eschatological expectation impossible for us today.[10] Werner, a faithful disciple of Schweitzer, tried to apply the latter's views to the early history of Christian dogma. But like his master, Werner believed that Jesus was profoundly mistaken, and he leaves it problematical how we can be Christians today if the Church was founded upon such a serious misunderstanding.[11]

Rosemary Ruether has been considerably influenced by Martin Werner, but she herself leans toward a futurist eschatology as Werner did not. She holds that while in some sense Jesus was the Messiah (Christ), in another sense he was not. At least he is not yet fully the Christ. Therefore the Jews are in some sense correct when they continue to affirm that the Messiah is still to come. To insist with Pannenberg that the end of history has already come with the resurrection of Jesus is, she asserts, to raise many difficulties. In Pannenberg's theology, she contends, Christianity threatens to become a closed ideological universe, in which the Jews "become the type of reprobate and superseded humanity."[12]

On the other hand, Ruether as a Christian holds that in some kind of paradoxical way the coming Kingdom reaches into history with Jesus and becomes the foundation of our hope and striving for an ever greater future. Thus her position is rather close to that of Moltmann, whom she nevertheless accuses of still using mythological language. With their heavy accent on the extent to which the eschatological future is still outstanding, Moltmann and Ruether come close to the futurist or consistent eschatological position, and this affects their ecclesiology. But as Christians they do find a certain provisional ultimacy in Jesus and his resurrection.

The opposite extreme position, likewise verging on the denial of Christianity, is a presentist or fully realized eschatology. All Christians confess in their creeds that Jesus will come to judge the living and the dead, and that they believe in the life of the world to come. They look forward in hope to some kind of future consummation, however incapable they may feel of articulating the nature of that to which they look forward. Whether they speak of personal immortality or resurrection or of a renewed cosmos or a new creation, or are reduced to apophatic silence about the whole matter, they are convinced that something lies ahead, that firm hope is not an illusion. They do not believe that what is experienced in the brief span of an individual's earthly existence is the whole of God's redemptive gift even to that individual, still less to the whole human family.

As representatives of "realized eschatology," C. H. Dodd and J. A. T. Robinson are usually listed. Dodd set forth his position in conscious opposition to Weiss and Schweitzer, emphasizing all the New Testament texts that they discounted. He seems to be asserting, in the strongest possible terms, that according to the original Christian community—even according to Jesus himself—the last times have already come in the Christ event, which gives the key to the meaning of history. But Dodd adds:

> While, however, the New Testament affirms with full seriousness that the great divine event has happened, there remains a residue of eschatology which is not exhausted in the "realized eschatology" of the Gospel, namely, the element of sheer finality. While history still goes on, a view of the world, which, like the prophetic and Christian view, insists that history as a unity, must necessarily represent it as having an end, as well as a beginning, however impossible it may be for philosophy to admit the idea of finite time. Thus the idea of a second coming of Christ appears along with the emphatic assertion that His coming in history satisfies all the conditions of the eschatological event, *except* that of absolute finality.[13]

Thus the image of the Last Judgment or the Second Coming remains in Dodd's assessment "the least inadequate myth of the goal of history."[14]

In later works Dodd admitted that his own term, "realized eschatology," was not an entirely happy one.[15] His main concern, however, was to insist on the essential completeness of history in Jesus, and to demythologize some of the New Testament apocalyptic, which he regarded as a lapse from the doctrine of Jesus to a pre-Christian level of Jewish eschatology. He is prudently skeptical about the possibility of overcoming myth in our talk about the Second Coming or the Last Judgment.

J. A. T. Robinson's position is basically similar to Dodd's except that he uses the term "inaugurated eschatology" rather than "realized eschatology." He denies the parousia as a separate and distinct future event, but he does not exclude the element of futurity in Christian hope. He holds that the Kingdom is still to come to completion; it has only been inaugurated.[16]

Apart from the highly nuanced exceptions already mentioned, practically all Christians hold some kind of partially realized eschatology. This would be the middle position. But it breaks down under examination into a number of subpositions, which may suitably be correlated, I believe, with the five types of ecclesiology already set forth.

In the institutional model of the Church, attention is focused on the deposit Christ is believed to have left behind him: the threefold deposit of doctrine, ministry, and sacraments. This deposit is an eschatological gift insofar as no greater gift can be bestowed within history; by itself it is sufficient to save men of every generation until the end of the world.

The Church is eschatological insofar as it administers this eschatological patrimony and, further, insofar as its entire activity is directed toward bringing men to their ultimate goal in heaven. The goal exists in the future. The world and man are in movement toward it. The Church is a kind of cable car or sacred chariot that takes men to their destination, lifting them over the abyss. If men stay aboard and avoid serious misconduct unbecoming a passenger, they may be confident of reaching their destination.

Since the Church, in this theory, appears simply as a means of grace, there is no real place for the Church in the final consummation. Heaven is understood as a face-to-face vision of the divine essence, with no social dimension. Because man's social life, in this model, is fully institutionalized, the disappearance of the institution at the end of man's earthly pilgrimage involves the termination of social life. Each individual, equipped with his own pair of opera glasses (*lumen gloriae*), gazes on the divine essence without being conscious of who is in the next box.

From the High Middle Ages until Vatican II there is little or no mention of the heavenly Church in official Church documents. The reason for this omission is the predominance, during this period, of the institutional model of the Church. Vatican II made a sharp break with this modern tradition. In reintroducing the theme of the heavenly Church it implicitly repudiated the primarily institutional ecclesiology of the Counter Reformation. It relied more on the other models to which we now turn.

If the Church is viewed as a mystical communion, its relationship to the eschaton is radically different than in the institutional model. The mystical communion of men with one another in Christ is something that begins on earth and is consummated in heaven. This implies that the Church, which exists inchoately in this life, reaches its fullness in the life beyond. *Lumen gentium*, as we have seen, says so in as many words. This is not a new invention of Vatican II, but a very traditional doctrine. As I have already indicated, many of the biblical authors see the Church within history as a foretaste or anticipation of what the Church is to be. Paul sees it as a temple still in the process of being built, a body still growing into mature manhood. The Apocalypse sees at the end of history the marriage of the Lamb. The Church enters into its glory when the marriage is consummated in heaven. The People of God becomes most fully God's People when it is gathered at the heavenly banquet.

The Church on earth, according to this ecclesiology, is not merely a promise or pledge of the heavenly Church, but is an anticipation of it. The Holy Spirit, the eschatological gift, has already been poured forth on the Christian community. Paul describes the Holy Spirit as the first fruits (*aparchē*, Rom. 8:23), the earnest or down payment (*arrabōn*, 2 Cor. 1:22, 5:5) of the fullness.

Throughout the Patristic period, Christian preachers and theologians looked upon the Church as the communion of saints that exists imperfectly here on earth and perfectly in the blessed in heaven. Heaven exists not only in the future but even now in the saints who have gone before us. The earthly Church, for Augustine, is only the inferior part of the total Church.

Medieval monasticism was concerned to achieve on earth the most perfect replica of heaven that could be attained. For Bernard of Clairvaux the monk should live here on earth the life of the blessed, undistracted by the demands of the body and all worldly concerns. To some extent this may have been an evasion of worldly responsibilities, but it was an attractive ideal that in many ways proved beneficial to culture. The high spiritual ideals of monastic theology permeated the art, architecture, literature, and music of the Middle Ages.

In much modern theology the idea persists that the communion of believers in the Church should be an earthly preview of the joys of heaven. I think we must agree that the Church not only promises to bring men to eternal life but even now gives them a share in that which it promises. This agrees with the "realized"—or, perhaps better, "inaugurated"—eschatology of the Fourth Gospel: "He who believes in me has life everlasting" (Jn. 6:47). The life we enjoy through grace on earth is essentially the same as that which we shall enjoy in glory hereafter. A very strong insistence on this identity can lead to a certain de-eschatologizing of theology, as in the case of Paul Tillich. Heaven can be conceived of as the depth dimension of what is already given in history. This view is not a necessary consequence of the "mystical communion" idea of the Church, but is quite compatible with it.

In the last three Assemblies of the World Council of Churches (Evanston, 1954; New Delhi, 1961; and Uppsala, 1968), there has been a strong emphasis on the idea of the Church as the pilgrim people of God still on the way to its completion. The New Delhi Report on Witness explicitly connected the pilgrim status of the Church with the necessity of ongoing reformation:

> A reappraisal of the patterns of church organization and institutions inherited by the younger churches must be attempted, so that outdated forms which belonged to an era that is rapidly passing away may be replaced by strong and relevant ways of evangelism. This is only one illustration, but an important one, of how the Church may become the Pilgrim Church, which goes forth boldly as Abraham did into the unknown future, not afraid to leave behind the securities of its conventional structure, glad to dwell in the tent of perpetual adaptation, looking to the city whose builder and maker is God.[17]

Something of the same vision of the Pilgrim Church penetrates many of the documents of Vatican II. Echoing the language of Augustine, *Lumen gentium* eloquently expresses this point of view:

> The Church, "like a pilgrim in a foreign land, presses forward amid the persecutions of the world and the consolations of God," announcing the cross and death of the Lord until He comes (cf. 1 Cor. 11:26). By the power of the risen Lord, she is given strength to overcome patiently and lovingly the afflictions and hardships which assail her from within and without, and to show

forth in the world the mystery of the Lord in a
faithful though shadowed way, until at last it
will be revealed in total splendor.[18]

A similar dynamic vision of the Church animates the
Constitution on Divine Revelation. "As the centuries succeed one another," says this decree, "the Church constantly moves forward toward the fullness of divine truth
until the words of God reach their complete fulfillment in
her."[19] The foundations have been laid, but the building is
still incomplete. The Constitution on the Liturgy reflects
the same point of view. It quotes Ephesians to the effect
that the Church is "built upon the foundation of the
apostles and prophets, Christ Himself being the chief cor-
nerstone." In him "the whole structure is joined together
and grows into a holy temple in the Lord, in whom you
also are built into it for a dwelling place for God in the
Spirit" (Eph. 2:20–22). Christians, in other words, are the
living stones of a temple that is still under construction.[20]

Theologians who adhere to these organic and community models do not always agree about the relationship between the development of the Church in history and the
final consummation. Some follow what René Laurentin
calls an "eschatology of continuity" in which "eternity—
which may at times actually lose its importance or even
significance in this view—is perceived ultimately as the
harvest of a ripe fruit from the tree of knowledge."[21]
Others look upon the final parousia as a catastrophic and
discontinuous event. Vatican II, on the whole, seems to
have favored the former approach. The Pastoral Constitution on the Church in the Modern World, in Article
39, which we shall presently discuss in connection with
our fifth ecclesiological model, emphasizes the perdurance
of human achievements on earth in the final Kingdom.

The third ecclesiological type, the sacramental, is in
some way intermediate between the two just considered,
since it recognizes both the distance of the Church from
heaven and the hidden presence within the Church of the
heavenly gift. Consistent with this point of view, *Lumen*

*gentium* in Article 3 asserts that the Church is the Kingdom of heaven now present in mystery. In other words, the Church is here described as the mystery or sacramental presence of the ultimate, consummated Kingdom.

In this ecclesiology, therefore, the church is seen as eschatological insofar as it is a sacrament of the eschatological Kingdom. The sacrament is in the first place a sign. By its visible presence the Church reminds men of God's Kingdom and keeps alive their hope for the blessings of eternal life. But it is more than a sign. It betokens the actual presence, in a hidden way, of that to which it points. What is essential to the Kingdom, the reconciling grace of Christ, is truly at work in the Church, although not exclusively in the Church. The Church, with the help of the gospel and of the Holy Spirit, is able to discern and celebrate the gifts of God to men. It assembles in manifest visibility about the altar of the Lord and proclaims the Lord's death until he comes. At the Eucharist the Church becomes more than ever a sacramental sign of the heavenly Jerusalem.[22]

The Church on earth must continually labor to become a credible sign of the future glory to which it points. It must be a source of hope to all who look upon it. Otherwise it would lose its savor; it would cease to be the eschatological sign that it must be as Church.

On this sacramental model, is the Church conceived as a reality that will abide when history comes to a close? Many theologians hold that the sacraments will cease, for in heaven we shall have open access to the reality that they obscurely represent. But it would be equally possible to maintain that there will be sacramental life in heaven, in the sense that the life of grace will be expressed and communicated by visible embodiments. What will be removed is only the ambiguity pertaining to sacraments on earth; for, as we have seen in connection with the sacramental model of the Church, it is possible on earth to posit the sacrament externally without the saving effect being achieved, reality being present, and conversely to have the life of grace without its embodiment in appropriate ritual expression. In the heavenly city this discrepancy will be overcome. Grace will achieve its appropriate expression, and the expression will never be fraudulent or deceptive. Man's experience of God will presumably be expressed through a whole network of tangible and social signs, and the sum total of these signs will constitute the heavenly Church as sacrament. Unless this were true, the life of glory could hardly be a true communion of saints, and the resurrection of the body would scarcely be intelligible.

This sacramental model correctly views the Church as a symbolic embodiment of the Kingdom. While acknowledging this, we should not be so taken up with this representational relationship as to forget the other relationships of the Church, some of which are better brought out by the last two models, to which we now turn.

Our fourth model casts the Church in the role of herald. Heralding is in several respects eschatological. First, it announces the arrival of the last times. As analyzed by C. H. Dodd, the Christian kerygma has as its central theme the announcement that in Jesus the time of fulfillment has come, and that men are to dispose themselves by repentance to receive the eschatological gift. The apostles make the claim to be the authorized witnesses of Jesus' exaltation as heavenly Lord and of the sending of the Holy Spirit.

Secondly, the kerygma is eschatological because it announces that the final consummation is at hand. Jesus will come in glory to judge all men, bringing history to a close.

Thirdly, the witnessing activity of the Church is eschatological because it helps to prepare for the final consummation. The Protestant biblical theologian, Oscar Cullmann, lays great emphasis on the statement of Jesus in Mk. 13:10 and Mt. 24:14 that the gospel of the Kingdom must be preached to all the nations before the end comes. So, too, in Mt. 28:20, the risen Jesus connects the missionary preaching of the Church with the "close of the age." In Cullmann's view, the Church's missionary activity is itself an eschatological sign. The period between the resurrection and the unknown date of the return of Jesus is, Cullmann asserts, the time of grace now granted to men. During this time all should have an opportunity to hear the gospel. The apostles, as heralds, are instruments of the eschatological plan of salvation. The era of the Church has its theological meaning as the interim during which the gospel is to be preached to all the nations.[23]

This eschatological understanding of the process of Christian mission is not exclusively Protestant. Vatican II's Decree on the Missionary Activity of the Church speaks in tones similar to Cullmann: "And so the time for missionary activity extends between the first coming of the Lord and the second. Then from the four winds the Church will be gathered like a harvest into the kingdom of God. For the gospel must be preached to all nations before the Lord returns."[24] The connection between Christian mission and the eschaton was frequently made by the Church Fathers and scholastic doctors. But it is interesting that St. Thomas shifts the emphasis from the kerygmatic to the institutional. What is required before the end time, he states, is that the gospel be preached *effectively* in every nation; and this means, with the result that the Church be established everywhere.[25]

Catholic authors, being inclined to identify the Church as herald with the institutional Church, tend to combine the fourth model with the first. Protestant authors tend in the opposite direction. For many of them, the theological reality of the Church consists in its activity of heralding the word more than in its stable existence as a structured organization. For them it makes little difference whether the herald be, in sociological terminology, a church, a sect, a missionary society, or a charismatically called preacher. With St. Paul these theologians might say: "What then? Only that in every way, whether in pretense or in truth, Christ is proclaimed; and in that I rejoice" (Phil. 1:18).

As already mentioned in our fifth chapter, many twentieth-century presentations of kerygmatic theology buttress the idea of the witnessing Church with an almost mystical theology of the word. For Barth and Bultmann, preaching itself is an eschatological occurrence. God—the true eschaton—is really present in his word. The word is charged with the personal power of him from whom it comes. The gospel, in this view, is not simply a word about God, but the word *of* God. The genitive is taken as subjective. The human preacher, like the Bible, is seen as an instrument caught up in the act of God himself coming to his people. Preaching that evokes the response of faith is the event that constitutes the Church, and the Church so constituted is itself an eschatological reality. It is not a mere event of secular history but one that has a divine dimension.

To be complete one must add that the word is a two-edged sword. It saves those who respond to it and condemns those who fail to respond. Thus it effects a judgment of discrimination. The eschatological reality is itself twofold. It is seen as implying both heaven and hell.

This theology of the word, as we have shown in Chapter V, is a welcome supplement to the traditionally Catholic stress on the sacramental aspect of the Church. But for the word to be truly eschatological it must carry with it the personal and living presence of God. In an adequate eschatological view of the Church, the theology of the word should be combined with a sacramental view and with an understanding of the mission of the Church to the larger human community, as pointed up in the servant model, to which we now turn.

The concept of the Church as servant might seem to be less eschatological than the views already discussed. Would not the Church best serve the human family by becoming totally engaged in making this world a better place to live in, regardless of any possible eschatological future? In some of the secular theologians, such as Robinson, Winter, and Cox, the eschaton as ultimate future almost disappears from view because of the importance attached to God's penultimate presence in the process of history. But other theologies of the servant Church take a strongly eschatologist standpoint. An example of this is found in the Vatican II Pastoral Constitution, Article 39:

Earthly progress must be carefully distinguished from the growth of Christ's kingdom. Nevertheless, to the extent that the former can contribute to the better ordering of human society, it is of vital concern to the kingdom of God.

For after we have obeyed the Lord, and in His Spirit nurtured on earth the values of human dignity, brotherhood, and freedom, and indeed all the good fruits of our nature and enterprise, we will find them again, but freed of stain, burnished and transfigured. This will be so when Christ hands over to the Father a kingdom eternal and universal: "a kingdom of truth and life, of holiness and grace, of justice, love, and peace." On this earth that kingdom is already present in mystery. When the Lord returns it will be brought into full flower.

Notable in this passage is the stress on the continuity between the values of human dignity, brotherhood, and freedom, to be realized within history, and their fulfillment in the final Kingdom. The world is seen as the arena where these values are to be realized, and the hope of the Kingdom is brought to bear as a motive for seeking justice and peace on earth. The figures of the fruit and the flower and the language of growth and development are employed. The thought and phrasing may have been influenced by Teilhard de Chardin, who showed a predilection for organic and biological metaphors, but a careful reading of the passage shows that the Council shied away from indicating the nature of the relationship between human progress and the coming of God's Kingdom. Thus it does not lend its authority to Teilhard's view that man's activity in building the earth is a vital ingredient of the future Kingdom, and a condition *sine qua non* of the parousia.

In postconciliar theology, both Protestant and Catholic, there has been a growing emphasis on the dialectical tension between the "already" and the "not yet" in the mystery of the Church. Pannenberg holds that in Jesus the ultimate future has already appeared, and that the Church is "an eschatological community pioneering the future of all mankind."[26]

> The Church is true to its vocation only if it anticipates and represents the destiny of all mankind, the goal of history. . . . Any narrowing of the universal vocation of the Church, any deviation from its character as an eschatological community, results in depriving the Church of its social significance.[27]

Moltmann likewise interprets the mission of the Church as servant in terms of his eschatological understanding of the Church.

> The Christian Church has not to serve mankind in order that this world may remain what it is, or may be preserved in the state in which it is, but in order that it may transform itself and become what it is promised to be. For this reason "Church for the world" can mean nothing else but "Church for the kingdom of God" and the renewing of the world. This means in practice that Christianity takes up mankind—or to put it concretely, the Church takes up the society with which it lives—into its own horizon of expectation of the eschatological fulfillment of justice, life, humanity, and sociability, and communicates in its own decisions in history its openness and readiness for this future and its elasticity towards it.
> . . . The whole body of Christians is engaged in the apostolate of hope for the world and finds therein its essence—namely that which makes it the Church of God. It is not in itself the salvation of the world, so that the "churchifying" of the world would mean the latter's salvation, but

it serves the coming salvation of the world and is
like an arrow sent out into the world to point to
the future.[28]

Catholic theologians such as Schillebeeckx[29] and Johannes Metz have been strongly influenced by the futurist
theology of Pannenberg and Moltmann. They too see the
Church as an "exodus community" pioneering the future
of the world. To this they add a strongly negative theology
of the eschaton: We cannot say positively what it is, but
we know from experience what it is not. The eschaton,
thus negatively grasped, gives the Church a standpoint for
prophetic protest against all forms of injustice and violence. The Church, says Metz, is "necessary as the *institution of the critical liberty of faith*."[30] Its task is not to
elaborate a positive system of social doctrine, but to be a
wellspring of prophetic, liberating criticism.

Having studied these various schools of thought, the
reader will no doubt wish to form some opinion as to how
the Church really is related to the eschaton, the ultimate
Kingdom of God. For my part, I do not feel compelled to
choose among the answers suggested by each of our five
models. One can accept certain points from each of them.
From the first model I would appropriate the idea that the
Church should help its own members work out their salvation by giving them guidance, admonition, comfort, and
every kind of pastoral and sacramental assistance. From
the second model, I would take over the idea that the
Church is not a mere means of grace, but a place where
grace is realized and lived even here on earth. The community of grace is an anticipation of the final Kingdom.
From the third model, I would adopt the view that the
Church is to be, here on earth, a sign or representative of
the salvation to which we look forward—a sign that is ad-
mittedly somewhat ambiguous in this earthly life, but one
that promises to become clear and unequivocal when the
final Kingdom arrives. From the fourth model I would
derive the ideas that the Church proclaims the coming of
the Kingdom in Christ, and that the proclamation itself is

an eschatological event, in which God's saving and judging power is already at work. From the fifth model, finally, I would accept the thesis that the Church has the task of introducing the values of the Kingdom into the whole of human society, and thus of preparing the world, insofar as human effort can, for the final transformation when God will establish the new heavens and the new earth.

The final coming of the Kingdom, I believe, will be the work of God, dependent on his initiative. But it seems likely that, as Rahner suggests, the parousia will not occur until human effort "has gone to its very limits and so is burst open by salvation from above by developing its own powers."[31] The coming of the Kingdom will not be the destruction but the fulfillment of the Church. More than this, it will be the future of the world, insofar as God's gracious power is at work far beyond the horizons of the institutional Church. The final consummation will transcend the dichotomy between Church and world. The glorious, triumphant Church will be indivisibly united with the renewed cosmos, "the new heavens and the new earth" foreseen by the prophets. And the triumph will not be that of a Church resting on its own laurels, but that of Christ who triumphs in his Church in spite of the weakness and sinfulness of men.

# VIII

# The True Church

In the course of history, there have been many Christian communities known as "churches," not all of them equally faithful to Christ and to the Spirit. This evident fact has made it necessary to distinguish between the Church as a sociological and as a theological entity. From the point of view of sociology, the term "church" would designate any group of men who consider themselves to be, and are considered to be, followers of Christ. Theologically the term "church" refers to the mystery of Christ as realized in the community of those who believe in him and are assembled in his name. To the Christian believer, the Church is not a purely human thing; it is not simply of this creation or of this world; rather, it is the work of God, who is present and operative in the Church through the Holy Spirit, in whom Christ continues his saving presence. Sociologically, the Church is a fact of observation, accessible to persons who do not have faith. Theologically, the Church is a mystery of grace, not knowable independently of faith.

Often the term "church" is used in two senses in one and the same sentence. Thus one says, "The Church must become the Church." Or one says, "There are many churches but there is only one true Church." The capital "C" is sometimes used to signalize the theological meaning of the term.

Because Christians approach the mystery of the Church in faith, they are concerned that the church body to which they belong (church in the descriptive or sociological sense) should be or become the Church in the theological sense. They would want to dissociate themselves from any body that was not, and could not probably become,

Church in the theological sense—a place where men would find one another and find God in Christ.

The problem of false churches is as old as Christianity itself. Since the first century, efforts have been made in every generation to establish criteria for determining the truth of Christianity. Today we frequently use as norms the four adjectives applied to the Church in the Nicene-Constantinopolitan Creed, still recited by many Christians at their Sunday worship. In this Creed the Church is called "one, holy, catholic, and apostolic."[1] Of these four attributes the oldest would appear to be "holy." The Church is called "holy" in the earliest forms of the Apostles' Creed, which contains the words "*credo . . . sanctam ecclesiam.*" As Nautin points out, the most basic form of this clause is probably "*credo in spiritum sanctum in sanctam ecclesiam.*"[2] The holiness of the Church is seen as a matter of faith, attributable to the presence in it of the Holy Spirit. The term "holy" was not ordinarily used, in the early centuries, as a criterion for distinguishing the true Church from its counterfeits.

The term "apostolic," on the other hand, was used polemically by Patristic writers such as Irenaeus and Tertullian, who maintained against the Gnostics that the Catholic doctrine was true because it was taught by those churches that stood in the apostolic succession.

The term "catholic," it would seem, originally designated the whole Church as opposed to the particular churches composing it. During the Donatist schism in North Africa, orthodox controversialists such as Optatus of Milevis and Augustine made much of the fact that the Catholic Church—the *catholica*—was a worldwide communion, as the merely local church of the Donatists was not.

Only in the fifteenth century were efforts made to develop for the Catholic Church a systematic apologetic that could be used against all possible adversaries. Ecclesiologists such as John of Ragusa and John of Torquemada, in controversy with the Hussites and others, based their apologetic for the Church on the four notes of the Creed.

In the Reformation period there was considerable discussion among Protestant and Catholic polemicists as to how to identify the true Church. Melanchthon and Luther in the Augsburg Confession acknowledged only two notes: the proper preaching of the gospel and the proper administration of the sacraments. In his treatise *On the Councils and Churches* (1539), Luther expanded this to seven notes:

1. The preaching of the true word of God.
2. The proper administration of baptism.
3. The correct form of the Lord's Supper.
4. The power of the keys.
5. The lawful vocation and ordination of ministers.
6. Prayer and the singing of psalms in the vernacular.
7. Persecutions.

In his polemical work *Against Hans Worst* (1541), Luther added still other notes.

On the Catholic side Cardinal Hosius in 1553 maintained that the true Church could be recognized by the four marks of the Creed. Bellarmine listed fifteen notes, but at the same time observed that they could be reduced to the four notes of the Creed. The catechism of the Council of Trent used the four notes, and, after some variations (reaching as high as the one hundred notes listed by Tommaso Bozio in his *De signis Ecclesiae*, 1591), the traditional four became standard in Catholic apologetics since Tourneley's work of 1726.

From the High Middle Ages until the middle of the twentieth century the assumption of Catholic apologists seems to have been that the true Church was identified with some one ecclesiastical grouping. The notes were used as a device for distinguishing between the true Church and its counterfeits. A somewhat different approach is indicated by Vatican Council II, which treats the four adjectives as attributes of the Church of Christ, to which Christians confess allegiance in the creed, rather than directly as attributes of the Roman Catholic Church.

After speaking of the Church under its two aspects as "a society furnished with hierarchical agencies" and "Mystical Body of Christ," *Lumen gentium* goes on to say

> This is the unique Church of Christ which in the Creed we avow as one, holy, catholic, and apostolic. . . . This Church, constituted and organized in the world as a society, subsists in the Catholic Church, which is governed by the successor of Peter and by the bishops in union with that successor, although many elements of sanctification and of truth can be found outside of her visible structure.[3]

The substitution of the term "subsists in" (*subsistit in*) for the term "is" (*est*) in previous drafts of the Constitution on the Church is one of the most significant steps taken by Vatican II. The emendation, with the explanation given to it by the Theological Commission, implies at least some distinction between the Church of Christ and the Roman Catholic Church, while at the same time asserting a positive relationship between the two. The meaning is presumably that the Church of Christ is truly present in its essential completeness in the Catholic Church, but that there is some discrepancy, so that the Roman Catholic Church, as a sociological entity, remains under an obligation to become more perfectly one, holy and catholic—and thus more perfectly the Church of Christ. The Church of Christ is not a purely ideal being—for it does subsist on earth as a historically tangible reality—but it is not unsurpassably actualized in any given community, not even in the Catholic Church.

Vatican II thus broke away from a merely apologetical approach to the four credal attributes of the Church, and opened up for Catholics the possibility of using the notes in other ways. In point of fact, the four attributes are differently interpreted by adherents of each of the five models of the Church we have been using in this book.

In Roman Catholic apologetics from the fifteenth to

the mid-twentieth century, the notes were usually understood in function of a highly institutional concept of the Church. The Church was statically viewed as a society having certain attributes definitively given to it by Christ. The institution was considered necessary in the sense that men were obliged to enter it if they were to have any good hope of saving their souls. It therefore became a matter of the utmost importance for ordinary people to be able to recognize the true Church. God, it was held, made it possible for anyone of normal intelligence and good will to do so, for he endowed the Church with certain manifest attributes by which it could be recognized.

All four notes were understood as characterizing a visible society. Unity, for instance, was understood as "the subordination of all the faithful to one and the same spiritual jurisdiction and to one and the same teaching magisterium."[4] Perrone, followed by Billot and de Guibert, went further still and inserted into the very concept of unity the idea of obedience to the visible head of the Church.[5] In conformity with this view, the Holy Office, in a letter of 1864 condemning the Anglo-Catholic Branch Theory of the Church, declared that true unity requires subjection to the pope: "Therefore the Catholic Church is one with that conspicuous and perfect unity of all nations throughout the world, with that unity whose source, root, and indetectible origin is the supreme authority and *potior principalitas* (Irenaeus) of Blessed Peter, the prince of the apostles, and his successors in the Roman See."[6] If that was the definition of unity, obviously no communion except the Roman Catholic Church could have it.

The note of catholicity may be considered second, for it is closely related to unity. In the institutional theory it too was understood as highly visible and measurable in terms of geography and statistics. In combination with unity, catholicity meant that the one Church, spread over the whole world, has the same creed, the same worship, and the same system of law. The immense outreach of the Church and the multitude of its adherents were considered to give particular effulgence to its internal cohesion and discipline.

The third note, holiness, was likewise seen as something characterizing the Church as a visible society. Hence the concern was not primarily with the interior union of the faithful with God, but rather with their visible holiness. Many apologists of this period put the accent primarily on sanctity of means, especially those means lacking among the adversary. Thus one finds long discussions of the value of the sacrifice of the Mass, the full quota of sacraments (seven in number), the vows of religion, and priestly celibacy.[7] In some cases the existence of an infallible magisterium was considered to give Catholics a moral guidance —and hence a potential for holiness—that was lacking to other Christian groups.[8]

The last note, apostolicity, was likewise interpreted as something belonging to the institution as a means of salvation. Chief importance was attached to the retention of the apostolic deposit of doctrine, sacraments, and ministry. For practical purposes, priority was given to government or office: for the office had the power to declare what were true doctrines and true sacraments. Apostolicity therefore meant for these apologists the legitimate succession of pastors, and the approval of the pastors was seen as coming from Rome. Du Perron and the Roman theologians held that communion with the pope is the formal element in succession. Whatever apostolicity other churches might have was therefore dismissed as "merely material." Apostolicity as a positive note therefore tended to be reduced to "*romanitas*."[9]

The apologetic for institutional Catholicism on the basis of the four credal notes was ineffective because the argument depended on an understanding of the four notes that only a convinced Roman Catholic—and not every Roman Catholic at that!—could accept. There was little basis in Scripture or in the early tradition for understanding unity, holiness, catholicity, and apostolicity as visible marks of an organized society.

Furthermore, the tendency of Catholics to rely upon

this type of apologetic for their own security in their faith had deleterious spiritual effects. The Church became to some extent a victim of its own rhetoric. In seeking manifest unity, the Church sometimes fell into a cult of uniformity. This period of institutional religion was the age of the monolithic Church, which aspired to a single universal language (Latin), a single theological system (Neo-Scholasticism), a single system of worship (the Roman rite), and a single system of government (the Code of Canon Law). Instead of encouraging new and diversified forms of thought, life, and worship, Catholics of this period tended to pride themselves on their exact conformity to Roman prescriptions.

In seeking to make evident its own catholicity, the Church at times fell into an irrational quest for sheer bigness, as though bigness could serve to authenticate the "little flock." The very notion of mission tended to be corrupted by an imperialistic effort to bring as many as possible into the fold. This goal was of course a necessary consequence of the institutional interpretation of the maxim, "Outside the Church, no salvation."

In seeking to manifest its own holiness, the Church tended to develop forms of piety that were showy and external. Catholics sometimes seemed to be counting their good works and "practicing their piety before men" (cf. Mt. 6:1–18).

The juridical understanding of apostolicity engendered an excessive concern with legalistic formalities, to the neglect of the spirit and of service. The idea that Christ had established the Church as a Society with some immutable form of government was responsible for a lack of creativity in meeting new situations. Instead of asking what had to be done for the sake of the Church's mission, Catholics tended to assume that their existing forms of government and worship were unalterable because Christ had imposed them for all eternity. Thus the Church became to some degree imprisoned in its own apologetic.

In the community model of the Church, the notes are no longer interpreted as the visible marks of a given society, but rather as qualities of a living community.[10] The Church is no longer exclusively identified with any one society or institution, but is seen as a mystery operative both within and beyond the borders of any given organization. Accordingly, the Church is described in dynamic, vitalistic categories, and is viewed as still in growth toward its full perfection. In the view of many authors of this school, the Church will not fully be itself until the eschaton. Thus its participation in the attributes by which it is defined remains partial and tendential until the end of history. The attributes are seen more as a task for every Christian community than as the exclusive property of one society. Yet the Church is present in existing Christian bodies, and for this very reason these bodies are called to become more perfectly the Church. The Church must aspire to be ever more fully one, holy, catholic, and apostolic.

The unity that concerns this type of theology is not the external unity of an organized society but rather the interior unity of mutual charity leading to a communion of friends.

The holiness that these authors esteem is not so much the holiness of means, nor an external holiness capable of being statistically measured, but primarily the lived holiness of an interior communion with God, pouring over into communion with one's fellow men. The extent to which individuals and communities actually share in the divine life is clearly known only to God. It can at most be surmised by men.

The catholicity that becomes important in this ecclesiology is not the accomplished fact of having many members or a wide geographical distribution, but rather the dynamic catholicity of a love reaching out to all and excluding none. This "catholic" charity makes the Church, in Bergsonian terminology, an open society.

The apostolicity that is of interest in such a theology is not the juridical succession of duly ordained prelates, but rather the perdurance of the magnanimity of the spirit that was originally poured forth on the apostolic Church at Pentecost. The apostolicity of the Church keeps it faithful to its origins and by that very fact prevents it from being merely backward-looking. This apostolic spirit drives it ceaselessly forward so that it seeks to embrace more and more peoples, to bring them closer together in mutual friendship, and to bind them in the diversified unity of a society patterned on that of the three divine Persons, whose mutual opposition in no way diminishes their intimate union.

In the third model, the Church as sacrament, the traditional four attributes may once again be used as criteria for the true Church, but the perspective is different than in either of the two previous models. The operative category will be that of sacramental sign. Vatican Council I, prodded by Bishop Victor Dechamps, among others, already set forth the idea of the Church as a divine sign having four attributes corresponding approximately with the four traditional notes:

> . . . the Church itself, with its marvelous extension, its eminent holiness, and its inexhaustible fruitfulness in every good thing, with its Catholic unity and its invincible stability, is a great and perpetual motive of credibility and an irrefutable witness of its own divine mission.[11]

Valuable though this approach was, especially in the circumstances of the nineteenth century, it may legitimately be objected that Vatican I was working out of an excessively institutional model of the Church. In the words of Latourelle:

> The First Vatican Council's formulation has doubtless to be understood in the sociological context of the nineteenth century, when the Church was conceived as a perfect, autonomous, transcendent society, which escaped the vicissitudes to which human societies are a prey. . . . The Church of the First Vatican Council seems

an abstract Church, an ideal Church with absolute attributes, rather than a community of believers on a journey, fragile and prone to sin. . . . Hence this formulation by the First Vatican Council lends itself with difficulty to apologetic use, especially in the context of the twentieth century.[12]

It would be preferable to approach the attributes of the Church along the lines already suggested in our fourth chapter. There it was indicated that Christ is the sign par excellence of God's redemptive purpose. The Church exists in order to make Christ effectively present as the sign of God's redemptive love extended toward all humanity. This implies the existence of a community having certain definite attributes:

First, the sign of Christ must be extended in time so that it becomes definitive and abiding, or, in more technical terminology, eschatological. In order to perpetuate the sign of Christ to the end of time, the Church of every age must remain in visible continuity with Christ and the apostolic Church. In other words, it must have apostolicity.

In the second place, the sign of Christ must be extended in space so that it manifests and actualizes God's saving will toward men of all regions and ethnic and cultural groups. Conversely, it must give expression to the response of all these peoples to the grace of Christ. This means that the Church must be catholic: It must extend itself everywhere and be realized in the conditions not simply of Western European or Atlantic culture, but of African, Asian, and Micronesian culture. As Vatican II said with reference to catholicity:

> This characteristic of universality which adorns the People of God is a gift from the Lord Himself. By reason of it, the Catholic Church strives energetically and constantly to bring all humanity with all its riches back to Christ its

Head in the unity of His Spirit.

In virtue of this catholicity each individual part of the Church contributes through its special gifts to the good of the other parts and of the whole Church.[13]

Thirdly, it is essential that the sign of Christ, thus prolonged in space and time, should be one that unites men with their fellows; otherwise it would not be a sign of redemption from the loneliness and hostility that plague men's lives. In the high priestly prayer of the Fourth Gospel, Jesus stresses the importance of manifest unity among all who believe in him: "I do not pray for these only, but also for those who believe in me through their word, that they may all be one; even as thou, Father, art in me and I in thee, that they may also be in us, so that the world may believe that thou hast sent me" (Jn. 17:20–21).

On the sacramental understanding of the Church, it is not necessary that the Church, during the time of its historical existence, should physically include all those men who live by the grace of Christ and are saved by it. Rather, the Church is called to be a representative sign—one that includes a sufficient diversity of men so that Christianity cannot be mistaken for the religion of any particular segment of the human race.

Finally, the Church must be characterized by holiness; otherwise it could not be a sign of Christ. The Church on earth will never be absolutely holy: "If we say we have no sin, we deceive ourselves, and the truth is not in us" (1 Jn. 1:8).[14] By reason of its formal principles, however, and under the leading of the Holy Spirit, the Church constantly works to purify men from their sins, to induce conversion and repentance. The very consciousness that the members have of being unworthy of their high calling, and of transgressing every day, is a testimony to the holiness that is congruent with the nature of the Church. The penitential liturgy expresses an essential aspect of the pilgrim Church. While the Church is made up of sinful men, from its highest officers to the most humble of its faithful, it is not related in the same way to sanctity and sin. It promotes the one and combats the other.[15]

On our sacramental model, then, the four notes of the Church assume far more importance than they do on the communal model. They have to be visible qualities of the Church as it actually exists, or else the Church would not be a sacrament of Christ—a visible expression of his invisible grace triumphing over human sin and alienation.

Visibility was required likewise in the institutional model; but an important difference must be noted. The first model called for a visibility manifest to the eyes of all, one ascertainable by measurements and statistics and capable of exploitation in a highly rational apologetics. The third model calls for the peculiar type of visibility proper to a sacrament as the bodily expression of a divine mystery. As noted in Chapter IV, a sacrament is a sign chiefly to those who actively participate in it, and is fully discernible only through a kind of connaturality given by grace. The presence of the Holy Spirit does not admit of a crudely apologetical demonstration.

Another important difference separates the use of the notes in the institutional and sacramental models. Whereas the first model uses the notes polemically to prove that one denominational Church is true and the others false, the third model would say that every denomination can be in some degree a sacrament of Christ, and likewise that each is called to be a better sacrament of Christ than it is. Thus, while Vatican I claimed unequivocally that the Roman Catholic Church already is an irrefragable sign of its own divine origin, Vatican II acknowledged openly that the Church, as sign, stands in continual need of refurbishment. According to the Constitution on the Church, the Church "exhorts her sons to purify and renew themselves so that the sign of Christ may shine more brightly over the face of the earth."[16] The Pastoral Constitution, *The Church in the Modern World*, says that the faithful, to the extent that they fall short of their vocation to holiness, "must be said to conceal, rather than reveal, the authentic face of God and religion."[17]

Then again, the Decree on Ecumenism declares that as a result of the failure of the Church's members to live fervently, "the radiance of Christ's face shines less brightly than it should over the world."[18] All these admissions are consistent with the Council's vision of the Church as a representative sign, or sacrament, of Christ's holiness as it encounters the lives of sinful men.

Our fourth ecclesiological type, which sees the Church primarily as a community of proclamation, would not attach the same importance to the notes as criteria of the true Church. The center of interest is shifted to Christ and to the gospel. The gospel, to be sure, is one and holy. Being directed to all men, it is catholic. Since it can never be changed into "a different gospel" (cf. Gal. 1:6), it remains "apostolic." The Church, insofar as it lives off the gospel, would share these attributes. The Church, however, does not proclaim itself; according to this ecclesiology it makes no claim to be an embodiment or sacrament of the gospel or of the Kingdom of God. What counts is simply the preaching of the gospel, no matter how sinful the preacher may be.

The Augsburg Confession, as already mentioned, speaks of two notes rather than the traditional four: the pure preaching of the gospel and the pure administration of the sacraments. The Church's sacramental activity is considered to be a sign of fidelity to the gospel and a kind of extension of it, a dramatization of the Word of God.

In this kerygmatic concept of the Church, no claim is made that the Church is an apologetically convincing sign or sacrament of Christ or of the Kingdom of God. The Church is considered to stand under the gospel and be judged by it. While admitting its own deficiencies, the Church is confident that in spite of everything the gospel will continue to be proclaimed. Of the four notes, therefore, the crucial one is apostolicity—understood in the sense of continuity with the faith and proclamation of the apostles. The sacraments and ecclesiastical office are subordinated to the preaching of the gospel.

Although evangelical Protestants generally recite the Nicene-Constantinopolitan Creed in their liturgy, they do not generally look upon the four adjectives describing the Church as manifestly visible notes signalizing the true community. Rather, these terms designate gifts that the Church is *believed* to have thanks to the promise of the Holy Spirit.

To specify the criteria of the true Church in terms of the servant model of the Church would be a stimulating task. The four notes, presumably, would be interpreted as characteristics of the new creation or of the Kingdom of God, rather than directly and immediately of the Church. The Kingdom of God is regarded as regime of universal brotherhood, embracing in intention all men and indeed the whole of creation. Thus it would be one and catholic. The Kingdom, moreover, would be holy in the sense that it is the gift of God, and that it unites men to God. In a certain sense the Kingdom of God might be called apostolic, if apostolicity means continuity with what God began in Jesus Christ. Since the Kingdom came into its own in the risen Christ, who himself became the first fruits of the new creation, every extension of the Kingdom is seen as an extension of the Lordship of Christ.

The Church, as servant of the Kingdom, would have a certain unity, holiness, catholicity, and apostolicity of its own. Its unity would be that of a team collaborating for the realization of the Kingdom. It would be holy insofar as it effectively dedicates itself to the realization of the Kingdom. Rather than the place where holiness is found, the Church would be seen as a catalyst of holiness in the larger human community. The servant Church would seek to break down estrangement and alienation, to reconcile men with themselves, with their brothers, and with God. Last, the Church would be apostolic insofar as it continues to labor for the extension of that which proleptically appeared in the glorified Jesus. In the words of Wolfhart Pannenberg:

> Only where the apostolicity and catholicity of the Church are understood as a matter of faith—

and not of a simple establishment of fact—only there can both appear in the Church's present. Then they will be the sign of God's coming reign itself, in whose service stand both the mission of the apostles and that of Jesus, and with whose coming the true, catholic, perfect society will be realized, in which there will no longer be any division between Church and political community.[19]

From the considerations offered in this chapter it seems evident that, while all Christians distinguish between the "true" Church and its defective sociological realizations, there is no general agreement about what the true Church is or how it is to be recognized. Most would admit that the four attributes signalized in the creed may be taken as criteria, but these four attributes are differently understood according to each of the five basic ecclesiological models. The most fundamental divergence is between the institutional model and the other four. The institutional model identifies the true Church undialectically with a given existing body, which is said to be "substantially" the Church of Jesus Christ. The other four models by their inner logic tend to depict the attributes of the true Church as ideals that are to a certain extent incarnated in history, thanks to the work of Jesus Christ and the presence of the Holy Spirit in the communities that accept Jesus as Lord. But these ecclesiologies would add that the Church of Jesus Christ is not perfectly realized anywhere on earth, and that any existing ecclesiastical body will be only deficiently the Church of Jesus Christ. At the end of time, the Church will be "without spot or wrinkle"; it will be the Bride fully adorned to meet her Husband. But as yet the bodies that go by the name of "church" all have their shortcomings and are to some extent vitiated by foreign elements.

Vatican II favored a compromise position. In agreement with the institutional view, it held that the one true

Church of Christ subsists on earth in the Catholic Church. In agreement with the other models, it admitted that the Catholic Church is itself an imperfect, and in that sense deficient, realization of the Church of Christ.[20]

# The Church and the Churches

Vatican II, as we have seen, made an epochal decision when it substituted, in Article 8 of *Lumen gentium*, the term "subsists in" for the term "is." The choice of terminology may have been intended to allow some scope for different interpretations. Persons wedded to mutually antithetical ecclesiologies could each understand the term in ways acceptable to themselves. From an institutional point of view "subsists in" could be understood as meaning "continues to exist" and thus as practically synonymous with "is." But in the context of *Lumen gentium*, Chapter I, which favors the sacramental model, the identity could be viewed as a qualitatively imperfect one. In the context of Article 8, moreover, the expression implies that something of the Church is realized in non-Roman Catholic communions.[1]

This raises the question of how the Roman Catholic is to conceive and express the relationship between his own communion and these other Christian bodies. Is he to say that Roman Catholicism, and it alone, is the historical embodiment of the Church of Christ today? Or that it is fully, and the others only partially, the true Church? Or, finally, that the Church of Christ is an inclusive concept that embraces, *ex aequo*, a number of denominations, one of which is Roman Catholicism? Depending on the way one conceives of the relationship between the Church and the churches, one will have a particular vision of what the unity of the Church must mean and how it is to be achieved.

A fundamental datum of the problem is that in some sense the Church must be one. As we have seen, it is so designated in the creeds. According to the New Testament there is and can be only one Body of Christ, one Bride, one flock, one new Temple, one new Israel, one new People of God. All these images connote unity. It would be out of the question for Christ to have several bodies, several brides, or for there to be several new Temples or new Israels. Jesus, moreover, prayed that there might be one flock and one shepherd (Jn. 10:16) and that all his disciples might be one, as he and the Father are one (Jn. 17:21). Paul gloried in the fact that Christians, since they know only one Lord, one faith, and one baptism (Eph. 4:5), are all members of one another (Rom. 12:5). So intimate is this fellowship, he delcared, that in Christ there is neither Jew nor Greek, slave nor freeman, male nor female (Gal. 3:28). All national and racial differences, all distinctions of sex, age, and social class, pale to insignificance in the light of the transcendent unity of the faithful in Christ. For the Church to be divided, Paul implies, is as impossible as for Christ to be divided (cf. 1 Cor. 1:13).

The unity of the body of Christ, of course, leaves room for a multiplicity of local congregations that may, in accordance with New Testament usage, be called "churches," but it excludes a plurality of rival and conflicting denominations that reject one another's doctrines, ministries, or sacraments. Almost since the beginnings, however, this dividedness has been the actual condition of Christianity. What is in theory abnormal has become in practice normal, and this anomaly calls for theological explanation. All major Christian traditions have had to grapple with the dilemma posed by the theological necessity of oneness and the factual givenness of division.

In this chapter I shall not try to give a complete discussion of this complex question, which has been the subject of many learned tomes, but merely to put the question in perspective by drawing on the five basic ecclesiological models already set forth.

The institutional model, taken in isolation, is the least favorable to ecumenism. In the abstract there would be nothing to prevent it from being said that there are a

number of autonomous organizations which, taken collectively, comprise the Church. But if one holds, for the
reasons just explained, that there is but one Church in the
full theological sense of the term, and combines this with
the affirmation that the Church is necessarily an organized
society, then it follows that no more than one denominational body can legitimately claim to be the Church of
Christ.

To anyone who accepts the post-Tridentine ecclesiology, as it may be termed, this logic should be evident. For
Bellarmine, as we have seen, the Church is essentially a society and essentially one. From this "it follows that those
who are divided in faith and government cannot be living
in one Body such as this, and cannot be living the life of
its one divine spirit."[2] The papal documents, to the end of
the reign of Pius XII, frequently deny that the term
"church," in a proper theological sense, can be applied to
bodies not in union with Rome. No other position would
seem to be consistent with the teaching of *Humani
generis* that "the Mystical Body of Christ and the Roman
Catholic Church are one and the same thing."[3]

Adherents of this exclusivist institutionalism will have a
distinctive understanding of the apostolate of Christian
unity. This was expressed in classic form in the encyclical
of Pius XI, *Mortalium animos* (1928), a vigorous condem-
nation of the ecumenical movement as it then appeared to
Roman eyes. The pope speaks critically of those who
would overcome the barriers among Christians by seeking
"fraternal agreement on certain points of doctrine which
will form a common basis of the spiritual life." Congresses
open to all who invoke the name of Christ, according to
the encyclical, cannot lead to the unity willed by Christ
for his Church, but are "subversive of the foundations of
the Catholic faith."

> Thus, Venerable Brethren, it is clear why this
> Apostolic See has never allowed its subjects to
> take part in the assemblies of non-Catholics.
> There is but one way in which the unity of

Christians may be fostered, and that is by furthering the return to the one true Church of Christ of those who are separated from it; for from that one true Church they have in the past fallen away.[4]

The institutional understanding of the Church, however, admits of several variants more favorable to ecumenical dialogue. One such variant would be the branch theory of the Church excogitated by Edward B. Pusey and other Anglo-Catholics of the nineteenth century. They maintained that the true Church of Christ exists today as three mutually divided communions—the Roman Catholic, the Orthodox, and the Anglican—all of which have preserved in its essential purity and completeness the apostolic deposit of faith, sacraments, and ministry. The branch theory was rejected by Pius IX. In an 1864 letter to the English bishops, the Holy Office asserted that there is no other Catholic Church than that built upon Peter.[5] For anyone committed to the Bellarmine view of the Church as a visible society, the branch theory could not be acceptable.

A second variant on the institutional theory—one that became prominent in the ecumenical movement in the 1940s—has fared better in official Roman Catholic teaching. This is the doctrine that the Church of Christ, while it exists fully in one communion alone, exists in a real but deficient manner in other communions, inasmuch as they too possess certain gifts or endowments of the one true Church. The Central Committee of the World Council of Churches, in its Toronto Statement of 1950, accepted this idea:

> It is generally taught in the different Churches that other Churches have certain elements of the true Church, in some traditions called *vestigia ecclesiae*. Such elements are the preaching of the Word, the teaching of the Holy Scriptures, and the administration of the sacra-

ments. These elements are more than pale shad-
ows of the life of the true Church. They are a
fact of real promise and provide an opportunity
to strive by frank and brotherly intercourse for
the realization of a fuller unity.[6]

More than a decade later, Vatican II, in its Decree on
Ecumenism, accepted this idea of a true though di-
minished realization of the Church of Christ in non-
Roman Catholic communities. It acknowledged:

Some, even very many, of the most significant
endowments which go together to build up and
give life to the Church herself can exist outside
the visible boundaries of the Catholic Church:
the written word of God, the life of grace, faith,
hope, and charity, along with other interior gifts
of the Holy Spirit and visible elements. All of
these, which come from Christ and lead back to
Him, belong by right to the one Church of
Christ.[7]

Vatican II, accepting this inclusivist institutionalism,
gave a certain limited recognition to churches and ecclesial
communities not in union with Rome as being of salvific
value for their members. It applied the term "church"
unhesitatingly to the Orthodox and to the ancient
Churches of the East. Without stating that there were, in
the proper theological sense, any Protestant Churches, the
Council did not deny this. Rather, it left the whole question open by referring to "the Separated Churches and
Ecclesial Communities in the West." Did the Council
mean that all except certain non-Protestant bodies, such as
the Old Catholic Church, were merely "ecclesial communities"? This interpretation would be quite consistent
with everything the Council says, but it is not the only
possible interpretation. It seems better to say that the
Council deliberately left the question open. On a purely
institutional view, it could be argued that there is not

sufficiently orthodox belief, sufficient sacramental life, or sufficient continuity with the apostolic ministry in Protestant communities to warrant their being called "churches."[8] But Vatican II, as we shall see, did not accept a purely institutional ecclesiology. To the extent that one follows the other four ecclesiological types, there is room for a more optimistic appraisal of the Protestant communities.

As we have seen in earlier chapters, many of the Church Fathers, from Irenaeus to Augustine, thought of the Church as a mystical communion. They saw the Church as wider than any given institution, and as present wherever the Holy Spirit is at work bringing men together into a fellowship of faith and love. This understanding of the Church as a communion is consistent with the ecclesiologies of the great medieval doctors, including William of Auvergne, Bonaventure, and Thomas Aquinas. After a period of oblivion, this point of view was revived by the Tübingen theologians of the nineteenth century, and has prospered in many twentieth-century presentations of the Church as Body of Christ and as People of God.

Protestant theologians have frequently sought to solve the antinomy between the necessary unity of the Church and the actual dividedness of the churches by drawing a distinction between the true Church, alleged to be an invisible communion of believers, and the visible churches, which are seen as man-made institutions. Paul Tillich made a sharp distinction between the "Spiritual Community," which he viewed as one and undivided, and the "churches," which he regarded as mutually disunited human organizations. He refused even to use the term "Church" with a capital "c," for he looked upon the "Spiritual Community" not as an organized body but as a mystical reality latent in and behind the visible churches. The "Spiritual Community," he would say, is really though invisibly one. The visible churches are not and need not be one.[9]

This type of dichotomy between the invisible spiritual communion and the visible, organized Church was many times rejected by the Roman magisterium. *Mystici Corporis*, for example, asserted:

> . . . We deplore and condemn the pernicious error of those who conjure up from their fancies an imaginary Church—a kind of society that finds its origin and growth in charity—to which they somewhat contemptuously oppose another, which they call juridical. But this distinction, which they introduce, is baseless. . . . There can, then, be no real opposition or conflict between the invisible mission of the Holy Spirit and the juridical commission which the rulers and teachers [of the Church] have received from Christ. Like body and soul in us, they complement and perfect each other, and have their source in our one Redeemer. . . .[10]

Holding to a perfect equation between the Mystical Body and the visibly organized society of the Church, *Mystici Corporis* taught that anyone outside the Roman Catholic Church is to that extent outside the Mystical Body. The Holy Spirit "refuses to dwell with sanctifying grace in members that are wholly severed (*omnino abscissa*) from the Body."[11]

At Vatican II, the preconciliar schema *De ecclesia* would have reaffirmed the coextensiveness of the Church as a society (*ecclesia societas*) and the Mystical Body of Christ. The Council Fathers, however, complained that the schema did not do justice to the mystical dimension of the Church, but reduced it too much to the juridical. Cardinal Lercaro, for instance, declared that in the existential and historical order, the societal and mystical aspects of the Church "do not always enjoy the same fullness of extension."[12] As a result of this and other interventions, the text was modified to acknowledge that the institutional or societal elements were really distinct from the mystical or spiritual reality of the Church, somewhat as the human nature of Christ was distinct from, and subordinate to, the divine.[13]

This view has important ramifications regarding the status of non-Roman Catholic communions. It opens up the possibility that, notwithstanding any institutional defects they may be judged to have, they may verify to a very high degree the nature of Church as communion. Even if one assumes, then, that the Roman Catholic Church and it alone has the "substantials" required from an institutional point of view, one cannot legitimately infer that it alone is the Church, or that it in every respect surpasses all other churches. The more important aspect of the Church, according to *Mystici Corporis* and *Lumen gentium*, is the vertical or spiritual dimension of communion with God.

Speaking from this perspective, even a Roman Catholic who holds that union with Rome is necessary for the institutional integrity of any particular church may still say that some communions not in union with Rome may, from a spiritual or mystical standpoint, merit to be called Churches. From this point of view—though perhaps only from this point of view—Gregory Baum declares, "Concretely and actually the Church of Christ may be realized less, equally, or more in a Church separated from Rome than in a Church in communion with Rome."[14]

Per se, of course, there should be a positive correlation between institutional perfection and spiritual perfection: The former exists for the sake of the latter. But in point of fact it may happen that the spiritual reality of the Church will be better achieved by an institution that is in some respects deficient. This is true for three reasons: first, the freedom of the Holy Spirit in bestowing his graces with greater or less abundance as he pleases; secondly, the freedom of individuals and groups who respond less perfectly to the graces given to them; and thirdly, the fact that a Church, though it may have an essentially correct doctrine and structure, may actually and existentially be very deficient in the way it proposes its doctrine or in the ways it utilizes its structures. Thus one may argue that, while the doctrines of a given Church really do correspond with what God has revealed, they are so badly stated and interpreted that they do not bring all the members of the Church into a vital community of faith; or that, while the papal-episcopal structure is valuable and even necessary, the actual incumbents are far from measuring up to the demands of their office. Hence the incorrect use or implementation of the right institutions could make them impediments, rather than aids, to the Christian life. Since the visible and external structure is intended to serve the mission of the Church, it has to be constantly judged and adapted so that it fulfills this purpose.

How, on the communion model, is Christian unity to be effected? Some theologians, who accept the dichotomy between communion and institution, maintain that the Church is already one, and that unity, in the deepest sense, does not have to be effected. In many World Council documents, the goal of the ecumenical movement is viewed not as that of establishing Christian unity, but rather of manifesting the unity that Christ has bestowed upon his Church as an inalienable gift.[15] But for those who would be more inclined to emphasize the necessary relatedness between the institutional and the mystical aspects of the Church, the lack of structural unity may be seen as gravely impairing the spiritual fellowship. Mutual love and service are deepened to the extent that Christians can acknowledge one another in Christ. To merit such acknowledgment, however, Christians must be truly responsive to the leading of the Spirit. Thus the two aspects, though distinct, go hand in hand.

From the ecclesiologies that look upon the Church as primarily communion, we can learn that the union among Christian bodies is not to be envisaged as if it were a merger among business corporations that coalesce for purely pragmatic reasons, but rather as a mutual rediscovery of brothers who have never lost their kinship. The unity for which Christians pray is not something to be manufactured out of whole cloth, but rather a coming to consciousness of a unity that, in germ, we already have thanks to the oneness of God our Father, Christ our Savior, and the Spirit who is their mutual communion with each other and with us.

The third type of ecclesiology, patterned on the idea of sacrament, leads to a similar set of conclusions, but lends them additional precision. This model, it will be recalled, distinguishes between the sign aspect of grace (*sacramentum*) and the reality signified (*res sacramenti*)—the latter being grace as something personally and freely accepted. The term "Church," according to Rahner and Semmelroth, signifies both aspects, but primarily, in modern Roman Catholic theology, it signifies the sign aspect. The Church, however, is not an empty sign; it signifies the reality of grace both within and beyond itself—the grace given by God, who loves, and wills to save, all men in Christ.

If one combines this theory, as Rahner did in his pre-Vatican II writings, with the idea that the Roman Catholic Church and it alone is the true Church, the distinction between the two aspects permits one to take a moderately favorable view of the status of non-Roman Catholic Christians. As Rahner noted, the invisible reality of grace (*res sacramenti*), for the sake of which the Church exists, may be realized more intensely in persons outside the Church than in persons within it.[16] The same would seem to hold for communities outside the true Church. They can be real communities of persons living, individually and corporately, off the grace of Christ. Even non-Christian communities may be animated by authentic love and thus partake of the reality of grace. A *fortiori* the same may be said of Christian communities external to Roman Catholicism.

Are we to say, then, that the Roman Catholic Church is the sacrament of salvation, but that the reality of salvation is to be found both inside and outside the Roman Catholic Church? This is what authors such as Rahner seemed to be saying in the early fifties, but this statement does not go far enough. Even if one uses the term "Church" to denote the sign (*sacramentum*), one cannot restrict it to Roman Catholicism. The sacrament of the

Church is constituted by the symbolic expression, in tangible form, of the salvific presence of Jesus Christ. This symbolization takes place through a multitude of actions, such as confessions of faith, the reading of Scripture, the celebration of the sacraments, and caritative service in the name of Christ. Groups of Christians who do these things are visibly consecrated communities of believers; they are believers who by their conduct visibly show forth the continuing efficacy of Christ's saving work.

In a remarkable essay published in 1949, Dom Jacques Gribomont, anticipating certain developments of Vatican II, discussed the ecclesial status of communities separated from the Roman Catholic Church. He judged them to be "imperfect realizations of the sacrament of the Church." Thanks to its sacramental life, he maintained, a dissident Christian community "retains a certain supernatural value, a kind of invisible consecration which distinguishes it from profane societies, demands a return to unity and produces its effect of grace in every individual member of good faith."[17]

On this sacramental theory of the Church one might be able to go further and assert that non-Roman Catholic communities may be in the theological sense of the term "churches." They are visible communities in which Christ is invoked and in which God is worshiped in the name of Christ. This fact alone gives them a certain sacramental status: They are signs of God's redemptive act in Christ, places in which Christian faith and charity come to a certain historical tangibility. From this point of view, one might hope for a less juridical and more sacramental approach to the validity of ministries in the various Churches than has thus far been prevalent in Roman Catholic ecclesiology. Is not a minister who feels called by the Holy Spirit, and who, by the consent of a believing Christian community acts publicly in its name, something more than a merely private person? Can one responsibly judge that his ministry is, in the famous phrase of *Apostolicae curae*, "null and void"? As we shall see in our next chapter, there is room in Roman Catholic theology for a theology of ministries that is free from the juridicism that characterized the Roman thinking of the late nineteenth century.

Let it be granted, then, that non-Roman Catholic churches are imperfect realizations of the sacrament of the Church. Some of them might even be willing to say this of themselves. But the Roman Catholic who makes this statement must be on guard against assuming too hastily that his own church is in all respects perfect. The extent to which any given church sacramentally embodies the reality of the true Church varies from place to place and from time to time. The Roman Catholic Church, like other communions, is always subject to improvement as a symbolic embodiment of the Church of Christ. Taking into consideration what has been said in the previous chapter about the sinfulness and reformability of the Church, we shall find it possible to agree with Hans Küng that no empirical church can absolutely identify itself with the Church of Christ. "Is this one Church," he asks, "being fair to itself if it overlooks the fact that in some respects it is not the ecclesia but merely a *vestigium ecclesiae*, and that what is only a vestige in its own case may be fully realized in the case of other churches? To overestimate oneself in this way is surely a sign of pharisaical self-conceit, self-righteousness and impenitence."[18]

From the point of view of his own tradition, a Roman Catholic will probably wish to say that his own communion has one feature that makes it in some ways more perfectly the sacrament of Christ than others—that is, a body of bishops in union with the Petrine See. The papacy, as bearer of the Petrine office, has served through many centuries as a potent sign and safeguard of the inner unity and universal mission of the Church as a whole. But other churches that lack this particular symbol of unity, catholicity, and apostolicity may nevertheless be in many respects admirable realizations of the sacrament of the Church. Some of these churches have preserved visible signs of apostolic succession in the ministry through appropriate liturgical rites.

If we follow this sacramental model, we shall conceive of Christian reunion rather differently than on either of the two preceding models. On the institutional model, there could be no possibility of organic reunion, but only of conversion. There could be nothing positively Christian in other traditions that Roman Catholicism did not claim to have in a yet higher degree. Thus all the changing and all the concessions would have to come from the non-Catholic side, in the direction of alignment with the "true Church." On the communion model, visible unity was considered unessential to the true realization of the Church or spiritual communion, although it was regarded as a desirable manifestation.

On the sacramental view, it may be acknowledged that Christian groups not in union with Rome belong visibly to the Church; for the Church of Christ is today historically realized in many churches, some of them not in union with Rome. These many churches, by reason of their mutual division, fail to show up the unity of the one Church, and in this respect they are deficient as a sign of Christ. For the unity of the Church to be achieved in a sacramentally appropriate way, there must be reconciliation among the churches; they must re-establish visible communion with one another. Christian reunion is therefore conceived not as the return of straying sheep to the true fold (as in the first model), nor as the manifestation of something that already exists in a hidden way (as in the second), but as a restoration of visible communion among groups of Christians that need each other in order that any one of them may become less inadequately the sacrament of Jesus Christ.

The fourth view of the Church—which, as we have seen, is characteristically Protestant—is also, not surprisingly, the most favorable to Protestant churches. Whatever they may lack by way of sacramentality, they are pre-eminently churches of the word. They venerate the Scriptures, confess the Lordship of Jesus Christ, and specialize in the ministry of preaching. As congregations of faith and witness they are in many cases more striking than Roman

Catholic congregations. In many parts of the world the most renowned preachers are for the most part Protestants. In the United States, many educated Catholics occasionally attend Protestant services and listen to Protestant sermons on radio and television because of the superiority of Protestant preaching.

Are these Protestant congregations "churches" from the standpoint of Roman Catholic theology? Are they realizations of the one true Church of Jesus Christ? The different answers given to this question depend very much on the ecclesiological models that are presupposed. If one conceives of "Church" according to the proper principles of this fourth model, as a community of faith and witness sustained by the active presence of the Lord, many Protestant congregations unquestionably deserve the name. The New Testament seems to authorize this usage by quoting the saying of Jesus, "When two or three are gathered in my name, there am I in the midst of them" (Mt. 18:2).

The Congregational type of ecclesiology that tends to accompany a theology centered on proclamation is not always deeply concerned with visible unity. Each congregation tends to be regarded as an autonomous, transitory, and imperfect realization of the Church of Christ, brought into being by the present proclamation of the word. In such an ecclesiology it does not seem urgent to establish firm institutional links among congregations, still less to merge them into the overarching unity of an institutional Church.

On the other hand, ecclesiologists of this school are quite conscious that the present dividedness of the Churches is proof of their failure to hear the word of the Lord. As Karl Barth expresses it:

> In the realisation of faith in the one Church
> in the face of its disunity, the decisive step is
> that the divided Churches should honestly and
> seriously try to hear and perhaps hear the voice
> of the Lord by them and for them, and then try
> to hear, and perhaps actually hear, the voice of

the others. Where a Church does this, in its
own place, and without leaving it, it is on the
way to the one Church.[19]

No one church can point to itself and say, "Look at me,
I am the true Church." Rather, in this ecclesiology, each
must confess that it has yet to become, in any satisfactory
sense, the Church of Christ. To the others each must say:
"Help me to see what I must do in order to be less false
to the reality of the Church." The churches can profitably
interact by mutually admonishing and correcting one another in the light of the gospel. No one church, even the
one judged "best" in its doctrine and worship, can be
taken as the norm. The only valid norm is the word of
God; and God's word is only dialectically or paradoxically
to be identified with the word of any man who purports to
proclaim it. Thus the way to unity is none other than
Christ, who is the way par excellence. Union is not to be
achieved primarily through interchurch negotiations, but
by the "continual conversion" of each of the congregations
to Christ, who is the source of the only kind of unity
worth seeking.

This kerygmatic understanding of the Church adds a dimension to ecumenism that stands to some extent in tension with the institutional, communal, and sacramental
views of the previous models. At the very least, we must
admit that this theory provides a useful supplement by accenting certain truths that the other theories tend to obscure. Taken alone, however, this ecclesiology relies too
much on the sufficiency of the word. Words by themselves can easily be unauthentic (cf. Mt. 21:28–32). Man
comes to fulfillment, expresses, and communicates in
many other ways besides. Preaching, therefore, is only one
of many elements in the Church.

The fifth model, depicting the Church as servant,
emerged ecumenically in the Life and Work Movement,
directed by the great Swedish Lutheran archbishop,
Nathan Söderblom. This movement was founded on the
premise that the divisions of Christianity would not be

healed until the Christian churches got together for the purpose of service to the world. The slogan of the movement was, "Doctrine divides but service unites." The Life and Work Movement is remarkable for its early recognition of the responsibility of the churches to the entire world and for the total life of mankind.

Since the 1920s it has become clear that the original slogan, "Doctrine divides but service unites," is something of a distortion. Christian service must flow from a shared conviction and thus in a certain sense from doctrine. Service in turn clarifies one's understanding of the gospel and in that respect feeds back into the renewal of doctrine. But the Life and Work preoccupation with service helped to offset an excessively static and abstract conception of doctrine.

Vatican II, as we have seen, to some extent accepted the "servant" image of the Church. The Decree on Ecumenism brought out the close connection between the service function of the Church and the attainment of Christian unity:

> Cooperation among all Christians vividly expresses that bond which already unites them, and it sets in clearer relief the features of Christ the Servant. Such cooperation, which has already begun in many countries, should be ever increasingly developed, particularly in regions where a social and technological evolution is taking place. . . . Christians should also work together in the use of every possible means to relieve the afflictions of our times, such as famine and natural disaster, illiteracy and poverty, lack of housing, and the unequal distribution of wealth.[20]

The same point of view is reiterated in the Decree on Missionary Activity:

> To the extent that their beliefs are common, [all Christians] can make before the nations a

common profession of faith in God and in Jesus Christ. They can collaborate in social and technical projects as well as in cultural and religious ones. . . . This cooperation should be undertaken not only among private persons, but also, according to the judgment of the local Ordinary, among Churches or ecclesial Communities and their enterprises.[21]

In an earlier chapter we have seen how post-Conciliar theology, both Protestant and Catholic, has accepted a more secular orientation. The Church is frequently viewed as an agent for the transformation of the world according to the pattern of the Kingdom of God. To the extent that believers of different confessions share a similar commitment to the values of justice, peace, freedom, and fraternal love, they find themselves drawn together into a community of action that transcends their present denominational barriers and paves the way for a richer unity in faith and worship.

Since 1966 there has been a great increase of collaboration for secular goals on the international plane. Organizations such as "Sodepax"—the Committee on Society, Development, and Peace jointly sponsored by the Roman Catholic Church and the World Council of Churches— have drawn up firm and realistic proposals for ecumenical action on behalf of the deprived peoples of the world. In the United States some of the most vital ecumenical activity in the past decade has flowed from common commitment to civil rights, fair housing, and peace. Robert McAfee Brown, a leading spokesman of secular ecumenism, declares that many Protestants and Catholics, when they march or demonstrate together for social gains, "sometimes feel closer to one another than do the uninvolved members of their respective communities back home. . . . If Martin Luther started a revolution in the sixteenth century that drove Catholics and Protestants apart, Martin Luther King, Jr., started a revolution in the twentieth century that is drawing them back together again."[22]

Lewis S. Mudge, another Presbyterian proponent of secular ecumenism, says that the presence of Christ is found "at the point where Christians, under the compulsion of the gospel, find that they can become creatively involved in the world's struggles, and hence have a presence to celebrate. . . . The presence of Christ in the secular environment is a presence 'in, with and under' outward structures and events. It is detected not by dispassionate analysis but by personal involvement, which, with the recognition of the brother, can become eucharistic."[23]

From a Roman Catholic perspective, Bernard Lonergan argues cogently that the Church is a constitutive and effective, as well as a cognitive, community. "It is constitutive inasmuch as it crystallizes the hidden inner gift of love into overt Christian fellowship. It is effective inasmuch as it directs Christian service to human society to bring about the kingdom of God."[24] The division between churches, he observes, rests mainly on cognitive, rather than constitutive and effective, factors. Ecumenically, therefore, it is of crucial importance for Christians to act together "in fulfilling the redemptive and constructive roles of the Christian church in human society."[25]

Many thoughtful persons who fully accept the idea of generous service to the world feel that this path is not a fruitful one for ecumenism. They would see secular service not as something specifically Christian but as a field in which Christians are on the same footing as non-Christians of good will. There is some basis for this objection. Christians should not limit their collaboration to their own fellow believers, but should seek in every possible way to join forces with men of conscience and good will throughout the world.

On the other hand, there may be something distinctive about Christian service. The New Delhi Report, issued by the 1961 Assembly of the World Council of Churches, argued that the Christian's concern for the world springs from an acknowledgment in faith that God freely loved the world, and is therefore a response to the God who first loved us. It is inspired by the example of Christ, the Servant-

Lord.[26] The Uppsala Assembly of the World Council, in 1968, in its Report on the Holy Spirit and the Catholicity of the Church, affirmed that the unity of man "is grounded for the Christian not only in his creation by the one God in his own image, but in Jesus Christ who 'for us men' became man, was crucified, and who constitutes the Church which is his body as a new community of new creatures."[27]

One might elaborate on these statements by maintaining that the Christian has a special vision of the inherent dignity of every human person, a distinctive ideal of unity and peace among all men, a unique concern for freedom, a singular confidence in the value of suffering and sacrifice, and an unequaled hope that in the end God will establish his Kingdom in its fullness. The courage, hope, and readiness to risk and sacrifice that should follow from a living Christian faith are much needed by the world in our day. It seems not impossible that Christians may find through cooperation that they are able to impregnate the world with these values. But if it should happen that Christians find they have nothing distinctive to offer, this should not keep them from cooperating with others who have as much to offer as they.

Before concluding the subject of this chapter, it seems important to note that the eschatological dimension of the true Church, considered in our two preceding chapters, has an important bearing on how one pictures the relationship between the Church and the churches. In some recent ecclesiologies, the true Church is seen as a project that is not and never will be achieved within history, though existing communities may well be places where the Church is *coming to be* insofar as they are being continually converted to authentic life in Christ. Edmund Schlink, in the opening paragraph of his celebrated address at the Lund Faith and Order Conference of 1952, gave classic expression to this point of view:

The Church is on her way between the first and second Advent of Christ. She is on her pil-

grimage towards her Master who is coming
again. She does not know what may yet happen
to her on this pilgrimage. Yet she is certain that
at the end of it stands the Master, Lord of the
World, and the conqueror of every adversary.
Then He will gather together all who are His,
from all nations, from all lands, and from all
ages, and with them He will celebrate the great
Supper of the Lord. Then, after all the struggle
and the strife, there will be one flock and one
Shepherd.[28]

Schlink's eschatological view of the Church, although it
had considerable influence on the pronouncements of the
World Council of Churches at Evanston in 1954 and at
New Delhi in 1961, has met with considerable resistance
on the part of Roman Catholic and Orthodox ecclesiologists. Thomas Sartory accuses Schlink of making an "es-
cape into eschatology," a "flight into the unworldliness of
the Protestant faith," and falling back into the pre-Christian prophetism of the Old Testament.[29] Without naming
Schlink as an adversary, Hans Küng warns that a prema-
ture recourse to the consolations of eschatology can under-
mine the efforts of Christians to overcome their divisions
here on earth.[30] The Orthodox delegation at Evanston dis-
sented from the majority report on the ground that the
unity of the Church should not be depicted as a merely eschatological hope, but as "a present reality that is to receive its consummation in the Last Day."[31]

These criticisms are not without validity. An extreme es-
chatologism, by conceiving of the Church as a merely eschatological entity, would overlook the conditions of the
new order of salvation, in which Christ has definitively established the Church as a tangible social reality within history. Nevertheless, it is true—and for this insight we are in
debt to the eschatological theologians—that the Church as
a present reality cannot be adequately understood without
reference to the eschatological goal to which it is tending.
We have seen how Vatican II, in many documents, asserts

that the Church will attain its full perfection only in the glory of heaven.

Alluding to the statement of the Decree on Ecumenism that the Church is still "tending towards that fullness with which our Lord wants His body to be endowed in the course of time,"[32] Heribert Mühlen correctly infers that the Catholic Church no longer understands itself as the static center of a perfect institutional uniformity, around which the other churches would be grouped (those having "more" elements being closest to the center), but rather it now sees itself "together with the separated churches as still on the way to the active realization and manifestation of that incomprehensible concreteness of the historical existence of the Spirit of Christ which will be made visible only in the total course of history."[33] Walter Kasper likewise has observed the ecumenical importance of this eschatologically oriented view of the Church:

> Far more important [than the question of whether or not separated communities are designated by the title "Church"] is a fundamentally new theological overview of the relationship between the Church and the churches, a view that no longer treats this relationship purely statically and juridically, but dynamically and in the perspectives of salvation history. The unity and catholicity of the Church are always and in every case still *in fieri*; they will always remain a task. The solution cannot lie either in mutual absorption or in simple integration of individual ecclesiastical communities, but only in the constant conversion of all—i.e., in the readiness to let the event of unity, already anticipated in grace and sign, occur ever and again in obedience to the one gospel as the final norm in and over the Church.[34]

The fact that Christian unity is an eschatological ideal should not deter us, but rather should motivate us all the more to seek its realization, in a participated and representative way, in the earthly form of the Church. The unity of the Church, as shown in Chapter VIII, is both a gift and a task. If there were no Christian unity, there would be no Church on earth; if there were perfect unity, the parousia would be here. As we labor in the interval between the foundation and completion of the Church, we must seek to promote authentic unity by the various routes suggested by each of our ecclesiological models. None of these approaches is invalid, none superfluous, and none by itself sufficient.

# Ecclesiology and Ministry

For practical purposes, all Christian communities may be said to have office holders or functionaries who regularly exercise a special ministry. It is difficult to discuss this special ministry, however, without prejudicing the results by the very terminology one uses. The various terms—such as minister, pastor, priest, and presbyter—are themselves biased toward one model or another.

The term *minister* usually connotes one who officiates at the liturgical service of word and sacrament. *Clergyman* is a member of the clerical caste, set off against the laity by ordination. *Pastor*—literally one who cares for the sheep —usually means one who governs a parish. *Presbyter* is not in common use in modern English, though the equivalent term "elder" is used by Protestants of the Reformed tradition to designate a certain grade in the ecclesiastical establishment. *Priest* is derived from "presbyter," but in content corresponds more closely with the Greek *hiereus* or the Latin *sacerdos*. These terms signify an individual set aside for cultic functions, especially prayer and sacrifice. Because all the vocabulary is tied up with particular ecclesiological models, it is important to emphasize that we wish to use the terms in this chapter in as neutral a fashion as possible.

The New Testament usage cannot be decisive for our terminology today, if only because the structure of ministry seems to have been different in different communities. In the Pauline letters (Romans, 1 Corinthians, and Ephesians) we learn of a great variety of services, functions, and charisms in the Body of Christ—but it is impossible to say which of these imply what we would call "offices." Paul speaks a great deal of ministers of the word, but much less of governmental offices. The Book of Acts gives considerable attention to presbyters and prophets. The Pastoral Letters, probably by a disciple of Paul, attach great importance to the office of bishop, without however clearly distinguishing between bishops and presbyters. A curious fact about the New Testament is the absence of any precise indication as to whether there were officers specially designated for cultic functions. The term "priest" (*hiereus*) is not applied to any particular class of persons within the Christian community, though the entire Christian community is designated as a "priestly people" (1 Pt. 2:9).

A historical study of the development of Christian ministry would probably show that the Church in every age has adjusted its structures and offices so as to operate more effectively in the social environment in which it finds itself. In a class society, the Church tends to become more hierarchical and aristocratic; bishops appear as princes of the Church. In a professionally organized society, ecclesiastical leaders take on the attributes of professionals. Churchmen are compared with lawyers, doctors, and professors; they study Greek and receive, at least *honoris causa*, doctoral degrees. In a media-dominated society, such as is emerging in our time, Church leaders may be forced to assume a more personal and spontaneous style of leadership. They will be judged on the basis of whether they can create powerful religious experiences, compete with TV celebrities, and project the kind of image that evokes popular enthusiasm.

Without seeking to probe all the exegetical, historical, and sociological dimensions of the problem, this chapter will explore the relationship between the patterns of ministry and the five basic models of the Church set forth in previous chapters. Each of these models, I shall contend, entails a particular vision of the ministry.

The primary analogue for the theory of the Church as institution is, as noted, the secular State. The cleric accordingly comes to be viewed as a member of the ruling élite—a public officer committed to the service of the institution and empowered to represent it officially. Under the impact of Greek hierarchical thinking, the clergy became a class that possessed total authority in the Church, so that no multitude or combination of the laity could exert even a modicum of power against the clergy. The clergy, in the perspectives of this theology, were thought to rule by divine right, just as in the secular State the kings and nobility were deemed to have their authority from God.

In the institutional model, priesthood is viewed primarily in terms of power. The threefold power of teaching, sanctifying, and ruling is concentrated at the top, in the pope and bishops. The bishop is given the fullness of hierarchical power, and the presbyterate is seen as a participation in the priesthood of the episcopacy. All the functions of the bishop or priest are juridicized. When he teaches, people are obliged to accept his doctrine not because of his knowledge or personal gifts but because of the office he holds. When he celebrates the sacraments, the priest exercises sacred powers that others do not have. According to some theories the priest's "power of the keys" enables him at his discretion to supply or withhold the means of grace, and thus to confer or deny what is needed for salvation—a truly terrifying power over the faithful. When the priest commands, he does so as one set over the faithful by Christ, so that to resist his orders is equivalently to rebel against God himself.

In defense of the institutional model of priesthood one may say that in a society as large and complex as the Church there is need for officers with a determinate sphere of competence, responsibility, and power. Without administrators designated in some regular way, and acknowledged as having certain well-defined roles, there would be chaos and confusion.

On the other hand, it must be recognized that there has sometimes been an overemphasis on the institutional element in the Church, to the detriment of effective service. The Church has at times become too much like the secular state to do justice to the spiritual mission of the Church and its connection with the mystery of Christ. Furthermore, the particular forms of government that have become established in some churches—perhaps especially in Roman Catholicism—owe too much to the political forms inherited from Patristic and medieval times.

Modern secularization and democratization inevitably call into question the system of clericalism that developed in the Middle Ages, and was perpetuated, partly for ideological reasons, by the Counter Reformation. There is no reason why a strong and efficient system of government cannot be combined with a large measure of lay participation and coresponsibility on all levels. The New Testament, at least, does not impose the three-tier hierarchical system (bishop, presbyter, deacon) today familiar to us. Theologians are coming to admit, in increasing numbers, that these hierarchical distinctions are of human institution, alterable by the will of men.[1] But any restructuring of the Christian ministry should be something more than a reflection of the contemporary *Zeitgeist*. It should take full cognizance of the biblical roots and of the special mission of the Church, as brought out by all five models.

Let us turn now to the model of the Church as communion. Vatican II, as we have seen, reacted against excessive emphasis on the hierarchical element in the Church and counterbalanced this with the image of the People of God. This communal concept of the Church calls for a concept of ministry as the fostering of fellowship. The Constitution on the Church favors this point of view when it says that ministries exist in the Church "for the nurturing and constant growth of People of God" so that all "can work toward a common goal freely and in an orderly way, and arrive at salvation."[2]

The Decree on the Ministry and Life of Priests attaches great weight to the pastors' office in building the community: "They gather God's family together as a brotherhood of living unity, and lead it through Christ and in the Spirit to God the Father. . . . The office of pastor is not confined to the care of the faithful as individuals, but is also properly extended to the formation of a genuinely Christian community."[3]

For some years before the Council, Yves Congar had been pressing for a more communitarian understanding of office in the Church. He has consistently maintained that the Church of God is built up by many varied modes of service, all directed to the common good. The "sacramental" ministries of episcopacy, presbyterate, and diaconate, he holds, are to be understood as modes of service helping the Church to develop as a living community of faith.[4]

Since the Council this view has become widely accepted in Catholic theology. A few instances may be given. Thomas O'Meara, O.P., writes:

> The priest must be freed and educated to recapture his role as leader or catalyst of a Christian community. That is what is happening in the many "floating parishes" to be found in the United States. The priest leads, enables, makes dialogue possible at all levels. He creates an atmosphere where meaningful sacramental worship can flow over into the equally important secular worship of God in men.[5]

Hans Küng, in *Why Priests?*, expresses a similar view. His description of the "Church leader" is the following:

> As inspirer, moderator, animator, in preaching, administration of the sacraments and committed service of love—he can keep the congregation together. . . . He will strive in every way for reconciliation and peace, but will also point out both imaginatively and soberly ways of joint action directed inward and outward, so that out of this joint enterprise the unification of the congregation is constantly achieved. In all this he is the gently effective guiding spirit (*spiritus rector*) of the congregation.[6]

One might ask whether Küng's "congregational leader"

ought to be called "priest." As a matter of fact, Küng prefers to avoid this term because of its association with other models. But he does demand a special vocation, commitment, and community recognition. He even accepts the idea that the community leader should be ordained. But ordination, he observes, is secondary to charism; it is the "public calling of a believer to the ministry of leadership, in which the Church recognizes and confirms God's calling."[7]

Congar points out that the modern idea of ordination as the conferral of a permanent power by ritual consecration is something that first appeared in the twelfth century. According to an earlier conception, to which Congar would like to return, "the words *ordinare, ordinari, ordinatio* signified the fact of being designated and consecrated to take a certain place, or better, a certain function, *ordo,* in the community and at its service."[8]

Like Congar and Küng, Walter Kasper describes the priestly office (he uses the term "priest") not primarily in terms of its sacral-consecratory function, but in terms of its socio-ecclesial function. The role of the priest, he argues, is the integration and coordination of all the charisms in a way that serves the unity of the Church. This charism of correlating the other ministries is itself a specific ministry.

With what is positive in this approach one can only agree. It is an excellent thing to emphasize, as these authors have done, the role of priest as builder and animator of the Christian community. But unless one accepts the communion model of the Church as supreme, it is not evident that all other priestly functions should be subordinated to this one. Theologians of this school do not always show a sufficient appreciation of the sacramental and mystical dimension of Christianity, and thus they tend to conceive of ecclesiastical office perhaps too much in the categories of modern democratic thinking. Küng, in particular, practically removes from the ministry the cultic element that has caused it to be called "priestly."

The third model of the Church, the sacramental, brings

with it the concept of the priest as a sacred mediator. The term "priest," questionable in some other models, is eminently satisfactory to proponents of this ecclesiology. In many religions, including Old Testament Judaism, this is a key notion: The priest is seen as a cultic figure mediating between God and the rest of men. Primarily a ritual leader, he stands in the sanctuary offering prayers and sacrifices to God, and transmitting God's gifts of grace and counsel to men.

Since the New Testament in several key passages portrays Christ as high priest and the Christian people as an essentially priestly community, it is not surprising that the Christian ministry, especially in its sacramental aspects, came to be understood in priestly categories. Not a few contemporary theologians hold that the Church actualizes itself most fully in its sacramental worship, and that the priesthood is the sign and guarantee of the eucharistic unity of the Church. Semmelroth looks upon the ministerial priest as the one who "brings the sacrifice of Christ to a sacramental, visible presence before the celebrating community. In their presence he is not only a guiding pastor and a prophet of God's Word; he is also the sacramental representative of the sacrificing Christ."[9] From a similar perspective, Roger Vekemans writes:

> The key point of priestly life, then, is that power not of evoking but of effectively bringing the humanity of Christ and the presence of God to the concrete present through the mystery of the Eucharist uniting a plurality of men around the table of sacrifice. It is a ministry that gives the priest a special dignity and manifests his temporal and eternal nature: eternal because he unites men with the absolute transcendence, and temporal because he exercises it within a given time-space community in forms that are constantly renewed for the present moment.[10]

Ordination, in this outlook, is neither a juridical action

whereby a person is installed into office nor the action of the community recognizing those gifted for special service. Rather it is a sacred action, performed with prayer and fasting, impetrating the grace of the Holy Spirit. The priest, thus consecrated, is supposed to be eminent in holiness, withdrawn from secular distractions, given to prayer and penance. His life-style must palpably express his dedication to God. Celibacy is justified on the ground that it sets the priest off as an "eschatological sign," wholly taken up with the concerns of the coming Kingdom.

A great deal of the strength of Roman Catholicism over the past few centuries has come from the attraction of this sacramental view of priesthood. This image of the priest leads to a high sacerdotal spirituality, and is felt to be helpful by many of the laity. If office in the Church is not to be a merely secular thing, but is to lead to an authentic encounter with God, the symbolic and mystical dimension of the priesthood should not be neglected. The bishop or pastor should not be allowed to turn into a mere business manager or personnel officer.

Like every good thing, however, the sacral concept of the priesthood can be exaggerated. It can lead to a superstitious exaltation of the priest as a person possessed of divine or magical powers. He may become removed from the rest of the community and surrounded with an aura of cultic holiness more redolent of paganism than of Christianity. Various clerical practices may contribute to this distortion—for example, the stress on living apart, on special garb, on a special sacred language, and on mandatory celibacy. The danger is that the priest will be viewed as a substitute for the community—as one who stays close to God so that the laity, relying on his intercession, may be worldly. This is a reversal of what is, of course, intended: namely, that the priest be holy in order to lead the community to holiness, prayerful in order to gather up their prayer, learned so as to give them understanding, and so forth.

In Roman Catholicism today we are witnessing a full-scale revolt against the excesses of the sacral concept of ministry. Rejection of this stereotype is one of the sources of the present vocation crisis in the Church. Still there are valid elements in this controverted view. The official representative of the Christian community needs to be united to God in prayer and faith, well versed in the Scriptures, and ready to sacrifice himself, as Christ was, in the service of others. As a focal center for the community the priest must visibly be a sign and sacrament of Christ. Catholicism has perhaps a special responsibility to keep alive this sacral dimension of priesthood. The idea of the priest as a living symbol of Christian holiness tends to be underplayed in some Protestant traditions.

For a fourth model of priesthood, we may draw upon our fourth type of ecclesiology. If the Church is seen primarily as a witnessing congregation, the dominant form of ministry will be proclamation. The ordained minister will be seen especially as preacher, and any sacramental functions he has will be viewed as a kind of prolongation of the ministry of the word. In much Protestant theology the sacrament is regarded as *verbum visibile*, a visible extension of the preached word, or a dramatic expression of the faith of God's people. The contrast between the Catholic sacramental view of the ministry, previously described, and the Protestant emphasis on the ministry of the word is well brought out by Karl Barth in his early volume of essays, *The Word of God and the Word of Man*. With reference to the Catholic form of ministry, he writes:

> At those times when the task of being *verbi divini ministri*, as we of the Reformed churches say, has worried and oppressed us, have we not all felt a yearning for the "rich services" (schönen Gottesdiensten) of Catholicism, and for the enviable role of the priest at the altar? When he elevates the Sanctissimum, with its full measure of that meaning and power which is enjoyed by the material symbol over the symbol of the human word as such, the double grace of the sacrificial death and the incarnation of the

Son of God is not only preached in words but consummated under his hands, and he becomes a *creator Creatoris* before the people. I once heard it announced literally at a first mass, *"Le prêtre un autre Jésus Christ!"* If only we might be such too! Even at the mass the Bible is displayed; but how unimportant, how indifferent a matter is the delivery of the sermon based upon it—and yet, again, how completely the poorest of sermonettes is transfigured by the saving radiance of the eucharistic miracle! For the sake of this miracle people actually come alone to church. How evident, obvious, well-ordered, and possible is the way of God to man and of man to God which leads from this center—a way which the Catholic priest may daily walk himself, and indicate to others![11]

Then turning to the Protestant form of ministry, Barth trenchantly observes:

. . . it is very clear that the Reformation wished to see something better substituted for the mass it abolished, and that it expected that better thing would be—our preaching of the Word. The *verbum visibile*, the objectively clarified preaching of the Word, is the only sacrament left to us. The Reformers sternly took from us everything but the Bible.[12]

But, as Barth goes on to say, the Protestant preacher is faced by a demand he often feels unable to meet. "The word of God on the lips of a man is an impossibility; it does not happen; no one will ever accomplish it or see it accomplished."[13] Thus Barth can challenge the Protestant preacher:

What are you doing, you man, with the word of God upon your lips? Upon what grounds do you assume the role of mediator between heaven and earth? Who has authorized you to take your place there and to generate religious feeling? And, to crown all, to do so with results, with success? Did one ever hear of such overweening presumption, such Titanism, or—to speak less classically but more clearly—such brazenness! One does not with impunity usurp the prerogative of God!

But does not the profession of the ministry inevitably involve both? *Is* not the whole situation in the church an illustration of man's chronic presumption, which is really worse here than in any other field? Can a minister be saved? I would answer that with men this is impossible; but with God all things *are* possible. God may pluck us as a brand out of the fire.[14]

The refusal of the sacred and the insistence on the unbridgeable gap between the creator and the creature in Protestant theology—or at least in some streams of Protestantism—makes for a certain kind of secularity. This is well brought out by Bultmann:

Luther has taught us that there are no holy places in the world, that the world as a whole is indeed a profane place. This is true in spite of Luther's "the earth everywhere is the Lord's" (*terra ubique Domini*), for this, too, can be believed only in spite of all the evidence. It is not the consecration of the priest but the proclaimed word which makes holy the house of God.[15]

Several contemporary ecumenical Catholic theologians have sought to bridge the gap between a sacrament-centered and a word-centered understanding of ministry. Karl Rahner in particular seeks to use the theology of the word as a starting point for the definition of priestly ministry.

The word of God, entrusted to the Church, he maintains, is in principle efficacious, and is not simply a communication of doctrine. The efficacy of the word reaches its summit in the administration of the sacraments. Thus one may hazard the following definition: "The priest is he who, related to an at least potential community, preaches the Word of God by mandate of the Church as a whole and therefore officially, and in such a way that he is entrusted with the highest levels of sacramental intensity of this word."[16] This position harmonizes admirably with the biblical notion of the word as an effective bearer of the power and grace of God.

Ratzinger follows basically the same line of thought. Commenting on the Decree on the Ministry and Life of Priests, he finds that the Council viewed the sacraments as actions in which the proclamation of the gospel achieves maximum efficacy. "This celebration [of the Eucharist] is the fully empowered proclamation of the Easter mystery of the death and resurrection of the Lord. In a manner exceeding our capabilities the Church is thereby led into the present of this mystery, brought actually into contemporaneousness with it."[17]

Following along the lines suggested by Rahner and Ratzinger, it may be possible for Protestants and Catholics to get beyond their sterile dispute as to whether word or sacrament is primary. In ministry we are dealing with a presence of God that transcends both, encompasses both, and gives power to both. The word of God is always somehow sacramental, for it symbolically makes God present, and the sacrament, which is the symbol of God's real presence in the assembly, never comes to pass without the word of proclamation. The official, or priestly, ministry is indivisibly a ministry of word and sacrament; and because it is both of these it can become formative of Christian community in a very special way. Thus this wide conception of priestly ministry includes that of community building. The three traditionally recognized ministerial functions of preaching, sacramental worship, and communal leadership should all be integrated in any complete theory of priestly ministry.

On the fifth model of the Church, it will be recalled, the Church has a responsibility not simply to communicate sacred doctrine, conceived as a special body of revealed truth, nor only to build up a holy community of believers living apart from the world, but rather to discern the signs of the times, to promote the success of the entire human enterprise, and thereby to help the world move toward its true goal in Christ. This ecclesiological model calls for a conception of priesthood that does not turn inward on the Church itself, but outward to the larger society of mankind. Such a conception of priesthood began to emerge in Roman Catholic thinking at Vatican II, which stated in its Constitution on the Church: "Because the human race is joining more and more into a civic, economic and social unity, it is that much more necessary that priests, united in concern and effort . . . wipe out every kind of division, so that the whole human race may be brought into the unity of the family of God."[18] If the Church is an agent of peace and justice in the world, it seems appropriate for the ecclesiastical leadership to point out the dangers of dehumanization and to inspire concrete initiatives for the transformation of human society according to the ideals of the Kingdom of God.

In recent Latin American theology there has been a strong emphasis on the need for priests to identify themselves with the oppressed in their struggle for liberation. An Argentinian priest, writing in the name of the Permanent Secretariat of the *Sacerdotes para el Tercer Mundo*, finds no reason to abandon the clerical status in order to engage in this struggle. "Latin America demands above all a salvation which is verified in liberation from widespread injustice and oppression. It is the Church that must proclaim and support this liberation, and the Church is in the eyes of the people permanently linked to the image and function of the priest. . . . We believe that our very commitments to man and the revolutionary process impel us to continue as clerics."[19]

With reference to the United States, Peter J. Henriot, S.J., takes a similar point of view. Addressing the National Federation of Priests' Councils on March 14, 1972, he spoke on "Political Responsibility as a Priestly Responsibility." He argued that "In the United States today, political responsibility as a priestly responsibility is integral to the mandate to 'go forth and preach the Gospel,' for it is directly 'action for justice and participation in the transformation of the world' [a quotation from the document "Justice in the World" issued by the Bishops' Synod of 1971]."[20]

The Bishops' Synod warned against "active militancy on behalf of any political party unless, in concrete and exceptional circumstances, this is truly required by the good of the community."[21] Henriot, in response to this warning, replied rather glibly that "these are indeed times of exceptional circumstances in the United States."

In principle, at least, there is no disagreement between Henriot and the Bishops' Synod. Normally the pastor's role will be to get the people to reflect seriously on their responsibilities in the light of revelation and to assure themselves that they are not violating the norms and values implied in the gospel. There are many ways in which the priest can have an influence on the social and political order. One of the least desirable will be for him to involve himself in active militancy on behalf of a given political party, for in this way he tends to give religious sanction to a movement that is subject to numerous non-religious pressures, and to come into conflict with members of other political parties who are perhaps equally committed to the gospel.

On the basis of the sacramental model of priesthood described above, Roger Vekemans takes a radically eschatological view of the priestly vocation. As the representative of Christ guaranteeing the eucharistic unity of the Church, the priest, Vekemans holds, must avoid aligning himself with any particular current of political action and must stand aside from the power struggles inseparable from politics.[22] This sacral and eschatological notion of the priesthood is perhaps too one-sided. By standing aside from political struggles, the clergy might effectually support an unjust social order or encourage indifference toward the moral dimension of public affairs. At any event, the differences of opinion regarding the relationship between priesthood and politics must be understood as consequences of the different models of the Church and of the ministry we have been examining.

In view of the variety of models, it seems undesirable to construct a single tight definition of priesthood. Priestly ministry is an analogous reality exercised in radically different ways by the functionaries of the pagan religions, by the levitical caste of the Old Testament, by Jesus Christ, by the Christian community as a whole, and by various officers within the Christian Church. The official or ordained priesthood, as generally understood, involves a certain recognized status conferred by ordination or its equivalent, though ordination itself may be differently understood in different models. Beyond this, priesthood involves actual engagement in service to the community—a service that may, in particular cases, be more prophetic or more liturgical, more sacred or more secular, more personal or more bureaucratic. Priestly activity—as the activity of the ordained minister in that priestly community we call the Church—may touch on any of the four traditional functions of the Church: community, worship, preaching, or caritative service. The fullness of the priestly office, which very few individuals adequately encompass, would include the building of Christian community, presiding at worship, the proclamation of the word of God, and activity for the transformation of secular society in the light of the gospel. These functions do not exclude one another, but they stand in some mutual tension, so that a given priest will not be equally involved in all four.

# The Church and Revelation

In all Christian ecclesiologies, the Church is intimately connected with divine revelation. If there were no revelation there could be no faith in the biblical and Christian sense, nor any worship, nor any Church. If people accept the Church at all, it is because they find in it a way of communion with the God who freely emerges from his silence and discloses himself to men.

Yet the notion of revelation is in our day highly problematical. For one thing, it is felt that many of the traditional presentations of revelation are mythical; they are based on primitive modes of thought that cannot be accepted by modern man. "It is impossible to use electric light and the wireless and to avail ourselves of modern medical and surgical discoveries, and at the same time to believe in the New Testament world of spirits and miracles."[1] Then again, men feel that revelation is something they do not experience. They are told about revelation by the Bible and by the Church, but reports about revelation are not themselves revelation. Our contemporaries, and we ourselves, are oppressed by the silence of God. Thirdly, some feel that the acceptance of revelation imprisons one in a ghetto. It leads to complacency, triumphalism, and disdain for others, and thus impedes dialogue with the rest of the human family. The absolutism of Christian revelation, and the corresponding commitment of faith, cut off discussion with the scientist or the philosopher, who maintains a continuously critical attitude of search. The acceptance of revelation seems also to separate one from the "outsiders"—those who do not accept the same revelation, or any revelation. The adherents of revelation, moreover, tend to turn in upon themselves and to lose interest in secular activities, dismissing them as "merely natural" or "merely human." Thus belief in revelation is sometimes felt to dehumanize man.

In the context of the present ecclesiological consideration, it would not be profitable to engage in a full-scale examination of the idea of revelation. It will be helpful, however, to show that many of the difficulties come out of an excessively narrow concept of what revelation is. My thesis will be that revelation, like the Church itself, is mystery—it is an aspect of the mysterious self-communication of God himself to man. The most adequate approach to revelation is through a plurality of models, and for present purposes these models may be matched with the ecclesiological types developed in previous chapters. In developing this line of thought, I shall be able to indicate in passing the types of Christology that go with the various models of the Church.

In Roman Catholic theology since the Counter Reformation the prevalent view of revelation has been strongly colored by the institutional view of the Church. The Church is understood as the guardian and conserver of revelation. As an authoritative teacher, the Church is compared to a schoolmaster—except that, unlike most schoolmasters, the Church teaches by the authority of office, rather than by giving evidence for what it says. To accept the word of the Church is an act of obedience to divinely constituted officers.

According to the official Roman documents of this period, the revelation authoritatively taught by the Church is a body of doctrine that derives from the Apostles, who received it "from the mouth of Christ himself," or "by the dictation of the Holy Spirit." This doctrine is fully contained "in the written books and unwritten traditions" that have come down from apostolic times.[2] Consequently, in the words of Vatican I, "All those things are to be believed with divine and Catholic faith which are contained in the Word of God, written or handed down, and which the Church, either by a solemn judgment, or by her ordinary and universal magisterium, proposes for belief as having been divinely revealed."[3] In this highly conservative and defensive climate, Catholics were compelled to assert, in the Oath Against Modernism,

> I sincerely accept the *doctrinal* teaching which has come down from the apostles through the faithful Fathers in the same sense and meaning down to our own day. . . . Equally I condemn any error which proposes to replace the divine legacy left to the Bride of Christ and to be faithfully guarded by her by any invention of philosophical thought or by any creation of human conscience which should by human effort improve itself and perfect itself in the future in unlimited progress.[4]

The conception of infallibility that emerged in this period of Church history corresponds to its highly juridical, authoritarian, and propositional understanding of revelation. On some presentations it appeared as though the believer had to give a blank check to the magisterium. Catholic faith was understood as an implicit confidence in the teaching office, and the test of orthodoxy was a man's readiness to believe whatever the Church might teach for the very reason that the Church was teaching it. One danger in this approach was that it engendered a certain indifference to the content of revelation. Believers were heard to say that if the Church were to teach that there were five or ten persons in God, they would believe it with as much faith as they now believed in the three divine persons.

While the institutional understanding of revelation still thrives in certain quarters, it has not received the approval of the leading theologians of the twentieth century, whether Protestant, Anglican, Orthodox, or Roman Catholic. The theologians who popularized the image of the Mystical Body contributed to the development of the notion of revelation as personal communion with God.

Emile Mersch, for instance, identified revelation with the illuminating influence of divine grace. The words of Jesus, he wrote, "are spirit and life, not because they are syllables and sounds, but because they are the outer, corporeal aspect of the life that communicates itself interiorly, the life of Christ, light of light who sheds light over those who belong to Him."[5]

About the same time, the Saulchoir Dominican, M.-D. Chenu, pointed out that the propositional aspect of revelation must be subordinated to its capacity to establish personal communion with God:

> The act of the believer terminates, truthfully speaking, not in the dogmatic statement, but in the divine reality itself, which the proposition expresses in human terms. Its object, then, is not a concept, formula, or system of thought, but the Person in whom I recognize the All of my life, the satisfying object of my blessedness.[6]

As we have noted in an earlier chapter, Vatican II in its Constitution on Divine Revelation gave strong emphasis to the notion of a mystical fellowship of grace. In the opening sentences of Chapter I this emphasis is clear: "In His goodness and wisdom, God chose to reveal Himself and to make known to us the hidden purpose of His will (cf. Eph. 1:9) by which through Christ, the Word made flesh, man has access to the Father in the Holy Spirit and comes to share in the divine nature (cf. Eph. 2:18, 2 Pt. 1:4). Through this revelation, therefore, the invisible God (cf. Col. 1:15; 1 Tim. 1:17) out of the abundance of His love speaks to men as friends (cf. Ex. 33:11; Jn. 15:14–15) and lives among them (cf. Bar. 3:38), so that He may invite and take them into fellowship with Himself."[7]

Revelation on this theory is practically identified with grace, and faith with the acceptance of grace. When a man opens himself to the divine illumination he becomes a man of faith. The general presumption among many adherents of this theology is that God is operative in a revealing way wherever there are men; thus revelation may be said to be present in all human knowledge insofar as it bears on the deepest values of life.

The value of revelation, so conceived, is not merely that of a means, as in the first model. Rather, revelation in this life is an anticipation of the final vision of God. It is valuable for its own sake because it is an aspect of the union between the human spirit and the divine.

Christ becomes on this theory the foremost recipient of revelation. His reception of revelation becomes the source and pattern for ours. According to Gabriel Moran, "In the psyche of the risen Lord revelation was received (or taken part in receptively) in fullness not only for himself but for all his brothers."[8]

In this mystical view of revelation, the Holy Spirit takes on a central role. As the Spirit of Christ communicated to the Church in the miracle of Pentecost, the Holy Spirit opens us up to look on the world with the eyes of Christ, and to see life as he saw it.

Compared with the institutional approach, this second model attributes far less importance to the official Church. The Church is seen less as a mediator or transmitter of revelation than as the gathering of those who have received revelation. God is immediately at work through his grace in the soul of every believer. Revelatory grace opens men up to one another. As men come to recognize one another as fellow recipients of the same grace, they gather to form the Church. The Church exists in some fashion wherever the divine mystery of redemption and reconciliation is at work. "Only after considering mankind as a whole and speaking of sin and redemption present in it, does it make sense to speak of the Christian Church."[9] The Christian community especially celebrates that embodiment and revelation of the redemptive mystery that took place in Jesus Christ.

This second model of revelation has great attraction at a time when many persons feel oppressed by the institutional structures of modern life, and are thirsting for an immediate, personal contact with the transcendent. It appeals to those who long for a human community in which love and trust can have a place. The dangers in this model of revelation are similar to those already noted in the corresponding model of the Church: that it tends to encourage the formation of little communes in which people enjoy each other, and undergo rarefied and beautiful experiences, but do not contribute responsibly to the development of human society as a whole. Secondly, this approach tends toward subjectivism and emotionalism; it discounts the objective, the doctrinal, the normative. Thirdly, it may easily foster illusions about the capacity of human communities to afford the kinds of satisfaction that humanistic personalism esteems most highly.

The third approach to revelation, which we may call sacramental, has arisen out of attempts to bridge the gap between the emphasis on the visible in the first theory and on the invisible in the second. It acknowledges two levels in revelation: the implicit and the explicit, the unthematic and the thematic. On the first level, revelation is an ineffable encounter, a pure experience of grace. This encounter, however, comes to expression through some kind of visible symbolization. Man comes to himself as knower by symbolizing what he knows in words or deeds, in creed or sacrament.

In the thought of Karl Rahner, the relationship between the two aspects of revelation is mutual.[10] The self-communication of God to man takes place in two dimensions: visible and invisible. Interiorly, revelation is the transformation of the horizons of the human consciousness, rendering man "spiritual." Exteriorly, revelation is the expression or utterance of what is apprehended nonobjectively. The expression, as symbol, introduces man into the heart of the unobjectifiable mystery of the divine.

Revelation in this perspective is essentially Christological and ecclesial.[11] It is Christological because Christ, as the Incarnate Word, expresses and communicates the unsurpassable self-donation of the divine. It is ecclesial because the Church perpetuates Christ's sacramental presence in the world, and is thus a sort of continued revelation. The Church is always revelatory in some degree, but is always called to become more revelatory than it is.

The idea of Christ as a symbolic revelation of God is well founded in the Scriptures. Hebrews 1:3 speaks of him as "the brightness of God's glory and the image of his substance." The Vatican II Constitution on Divine Revelation declared: "To see Jesus is to see His Father (Jn. 14:9). For this reason Jesus perfected revelation by fulfilling it through His whole work of making Himself present and manifesting Himself: through His words and deeds, His signs and wonders, but especially through His death and glorious resurrection from the dead and the final sending of the Spirit of truth."[12]

If Christ as sacrament is the culminating self-revelation of God, it follows that the Church, to the extent that it is the sacrament of Christ, is also a kind of concrete revelation of the divine. All the Vatican II texts on the Church as sacrament thus become available for the theory of revelation.

This approach to revelation bears some analogy to the kinds of communication analyzed in aesthetics. The artist completes his own experience in conceiving and producing his poem, his music, his work of art, and others contemplating the product refresh and intensify their own experience.

Adherents of this view of revelation can attribute to the Church a certain kind of infallibility, though not exactly the same as that familiar to us from the first model. Thanks to the abiding influence of Christ, and the promised assistance of the Holy Spirit, many Christians believe that the Church will always remain as a sign of the redemptive love that God has manifested in Christ. The perseverance of the Church in the truth of the gospel gives it a certain qualified infallibility, without necessarily guaranteeing every proposition set forth by the teaching authorities, even in their most solemn acts.

This sacramental approach to revelation has wide appeal in our time because many feel the inadequacies of the juridical and propositional approach of the first model without wishing to take flight into the amorphous mysticism to which the second is subject. The chief weakness of this theory, and of the corresponding model of the Church, is that it may lend itself to a certain aestheticism. This charge is particularly pressed by adherents of our fifth theory, who give high priority to social action.

The kerygmatic theory of revelation is that which corresponds to the model of the Church as witnessing congregation. This theory is represented in various ways by Luther, Barth, Bultmann, and by biblical theologians such as Cullmann. Concentrating on word rather than sacrament, this theology designates revelation as the word of God. Barth holds that the word of God occurs in three forms: as incarnate word (Christ), as written word (the Bible), and as proclaimed word (preaching based on Christ as attested by the Bible). According to which of the three forms a given author emphasizes, the word may be conceived more personalistically, more biblically, or more kerygmatically.

This view of revelation has its unquestioned center in Jesus Christ, who is himself the word of God. He is seen as the great witness of God's loving mercy and as the first herald of the New Covenant. His life, death, and resurrection are interpreted as wondrous confirmations of the words that he spoke.

The Church in this theory appears as the herald or mediator of revelation. Nothing else about the Church is considered really important. Its task is to be the place where Christian revelation is heralded and believed. The Church is necessary for salvation, for the gospel must on all accounts be preached.

> But how are men to call upon him in whom they have not believed? And how are they to believe in him of whom they have never heard? And how are they to hear without a preacher?

And how can men preach unless they are sent?
As it is written, "How beautiful are the feet of
those who preach the good news!" But they have
not all heeded the gospel; for Isaiah says, "Lord,
who has believed what he has heard from us?"
So faith comes from what is heard, and what is
heard comes by the preaching of Christ.[13]

Until about the middle of the present century, most
proponents of this theory of revelation emphasized the priority of words over deeds. But under the prodding of Old
Testament scholars such as G. Ernest Wright and Gerhard
von Rad, some today insist that revelation occurs primarily
in deeds and only secondarily in words, which are the record of the great deeds of God. For these theologians,
revelation consists chiefly in the mighty acts of God in salvation history. Regarding the dealings of God with the
Israelites as unique and unparalleled, they look to the
Bible as a reliable account of these deeds. Thus in practice
they do not radically disagree with those who find revelation primarily in the written words of the Bible.

The leading proponents of this kerygmatic theology of
revelation, mostly Protestants, consider that the Church
will always remain, thanks to the promises of God, as a
center of faith and witness. They insist, however, that the
preaching of the Church and all ecclesiastical tradition
must be measured by the norm of Scripture. They would
see the Church not as infallible in the ordinary sense, but
as subject to correction and as continually in need of
reform.

Bultmann's existential theology is, like Barth's theology
of the word, kerygmatic in orientation. But the difference
is very great. Bultmann severs the links between the
kerygma and history and holds that revelation consists not
in information about what God has already done in Jesus,
but rather in the event of proclamation itself. The preaching of Jesus as risen Lord, he holds, brings about an existential transformation of the hearer and opens up to him
the possibility of authentic existence. Bultmann has excel-

lent things to say about how the preaching of the Church today can deliver man from his fears, his pettiness, his selfishness, and give him courage to rise to his full stature as a man. Bultmann's critics, however, point out that unless Jesus historically existed and did the kind of things the New Testament attributes to him, Christian preaching would not be able to produce its saving effect, and would not even deserve to be taken seriously.[14]

The Kerygmatic view of revelation, in the various forms we have discussed, has had a very important impact on contemporary theology as a whole, Catholic as well as Protestant. This influence is palpable in the Vatican II Constitution on Divine Revelation, four of whose six chapters are devoted to the Bible. According to this Constitution, "all the preaching of the Church must be nourished and ruled by sacred Scripture. For in the sacred books, the Father who is in heaven meets his children with great love and speaks with them; and the force and power of the word of God is so great that it remains the support and energy of the Church, the pure and perennial source of spiritual life."[15]

Where kerygmatic theology avoids a narrow biblicism, as it does in the teaching of the major theologians we have mentioned, it may be welcomed as a healthy development. It is particularly helpful for Catholics, many of whom are seeking a path back to a more biblical and Christocentric theology of revelation, as a corrective to the ecclesiocentric theology of the past few centuries. This kerygmatic approach, however, would stand to gain considerably if it could assimilate the theocentric input of the second model and the sacramental emphasis of the third. Otherwise there is a risk that the theology of revelation may become too extrinsic, too word-centered, too authoritarian, too unappreciative of nonChristian religious experience, and too apathetic to the great events of secular history.

The fifth strand of revelation theology is at the opposite extreme from the fourth and originates partly as a reaction against it. The feeling is that with their strong emphasis on the special character of Jesus of Nazareth and of the biblical message, Christians are isolating themselves from many of the good things that are going on in the universe —things that should likewise be attributed to God and should be of help for Christianity's own self-understanding.

Corresponding to the servant view of the Church, therefore, a more cosmic revelation theology has emerged. Influenced by Teilhard de Chardin, some representatives of this school see Christ as the Omega force working throughout creation, present as an operative energy in the universe. Besides Christians, adherents of other religions and ideologies participate in this divine energy, and in that sense revelation is at work in and through them. Revelation is viewed on the analogy of an evolutionary force whereby higher states of consciousness emerge from lower states. In Christ, it is believed, creation took an immense step forward to its ultimate goal. His resurrection is seen as an anticipation of the ultimate transformation of man and the universe. Until the parousia, Christ is secretly at work in all creation, drawing it forward to himself. The content of revelation, therefore, is the inbreaking of the divine into history—the self-manifestation, so to speak, of the Kingdom of God.

Something of this theology of revelation is to be found in Vatican II's Pastoral Constitution on the Church in the Modern World, which declares that "all believers of whatever religion have always heard His [God's] revealing voice in the discourse of creatures."[16] As for the central place of Christ, it is repeatedly affirmed in passages such as the following:

> For God's Word, by whom all things were made, was Himself made flesh so that as perfect man He might save all men and sum up all things in Himself. The Lord is the goal of human history, the focal point of the longings of history and of civilization, the center of the human race, the joy of every heart, and the answer to all its yearnings. . . .

The Lord Himself speaks: "Behold, I come quickly! And my reward is with me, to render to each one according to his works. I am the Alpha and Omega, the first and the last, the beginning and the end" (Apoc. 22:12–13).[17]

The role of the Church in this cosmic theology of revelation is not simply to proclaim the biblical message to the world, but rather to enter into dialogue with all men of good will, to discern the signs of the times, and to interpret the many voices of our age, judging them in the light of the divine Word.[18] It is taken for granted in this theory, as contrasted with the first and fourth types of revelation theology, that revelation is an ongoing thing. As the universe is being Christified (to use the Teilhardian term), the revelation of God in Christ becomes clearer; new aspects of the mystery of Christ are continually being manifested.

The value of revelation, in this cosmic outlook, is not simply to bring the individual believer to his eternal salvation, but to contribute to the realization in the world of the values of the kingdom of God: justice, freedom, plenty, brotherhood, and the like. The Church, according to the Pastoral Constitution, seeks to consolidate the human community according to divine revelation.[19] As Christ was the "man for others," so must the Church become fully altruistic.

The strengths and weaknesses of this fifth approach are just the opposite of the fourth. Its strength is that it facilitates communion with all men everywhere, and eliminates many of the barriers that have made communication difficult. Its weakness is that it may tend to dissolve too much of what is distinctive to Christianity. Christians who are inclined to this theory have constantly to ask themselves whether they have any clear message, whether they stand for anything definite that they could not stand for without Christ. Is revelation really necessary for man to accept the value of peace, justice, brotherhood, and freedom? Could not a Feuerbachian atheist be as effectively dedicated to these things as a Christian? Is not the whole Christian teaching about preaching and sacraments rather a burden than a help in bringing about a community of the spirit that cuts across the barriers among the traditional religions?

These questions are posed not as unanswerable objections but as indications that the fifth strand of revelation theology, if it is to remain recognizably Christian, must include elements from each of the other four. In secular theologians such as Metz, Moltmann, and Pannenberg one finds a revelation theology that is secular and dialogic in orientation, but solicitous to preserve the unique values of Christ, of the Christian Scriptures, and of sacramental and ecclesial life.

In nearly all Christian theories of revelation, allowance is made for the discrepancy between the present interim situation and the final eschatological fullness, when revelation will be given in total splendor. There are different views regarding the Church's relationship to the revelation of the end time. Adherents of the first theory, and many adherents of the fourth, would maintain that the Church ceases to exist in the eschaton, and that the heavenly revelation will be an individual encounter with God or with Christ, independently of the Church. If one follows the second model of revelation theology, one will be inclined to say that the heavenly Church will be a communion in which all the members will find one another in Christ as head and vivifier of the Mystical Body. The glorious Church will join in a great hymn of praise at the eternal marriage of the Lamb. According to the third approach, the Church in heaven will be a true sacramental presence, or symbolic embodiment, of revelation, purified of the ambiguities that affect the Church in its present state of exile. In the fifth style of revelation theology, the final epiphany will be mediated not simply by the Church but by the new creation—the "new heavens and the new earth" (Is. 65:17, 66:22; 2 Pt. 3:13; Apoc. 21:1)—in which God will be "everything to every one" (1 Cor. 15:28).

Whether the eschatological revelation will be a smooth transition, superabundantly fulfilling the revelation already given in time, or a sudden and astonishing reversal, has been a matter of debate since Old Testament times. Between the optimistic confidence of the evolutionists and the cosmic pessimism of the apocalypticists no harmonization is possible. I suspect that the theories that call for pure continuity and for pure discontinuity are both in error, but that we cannot predict from within history the measure of permanence and of novelty.

# XII

# The Evaluation of Models

In all the previous chapters we have been engaged in what
Bernard Lonergan might call dialectic as distinct from
doctrinal theology.[1] We have been exploring the basic
models of the Church that have arisen in history as a result of the differing points of view or horizons of believers
and theologians of different ages and cultures. Each of the
models, self-evidently, has its own uses and limitations.
We must now face the problem, to what extent are the
models compatible or incompatible? Are the differences of
horizon mutually exclusive or mutually complementary?
Are all the models equally good, or are some superior to
others? Are they an opaque screen that shuts off the reality of the Church, or a transparent screen that permits us
to grasp the Church as it really is? If the latter, what really is the Church? What is the best model?

The critique and choice of models depends, or should
depend, on criteria. But here lies the rub. On reflection it
becomes apparent that most of the criteria presuppose or
imply a choice of values. The values, in turn, presuppose a
certain understanding of the realities of faith. If one
stands committed to a given model it is relatively easy to
establish criteria by which that model is to be preferred to
others. Each theologian's criteria therefore tend to buttress
his own preferred models. Communication is impeded by
the fact that the arguments in favor of one's own preferred model are generally circular: They presuppose the
very point at issue.

Some examples will make this clearer. Persons drawn to
the institutional model will show a particularly high regard
for values such as conceptual clarity, respect for consti-

tuted authority, law and order. They reject other models, and perhaps especially the second, as being too vague, mystical, and subjective. Partisans of the communion model, on the other hand, find the institutional outlook too rationalistic, ecclesiocentric, and rigid. They label it triumphalist, juridicist, and clericalist. An analogous dispute arises between champions of the third and fourth models. Adherents of the sacramental ecclesiology, appealing to the principle of incarnation, find the kerygmatic theologies too exclusively centered on the word; whereas kerygmatic theologians find the sacramental model too complacent and insufficiently prophetic. Promoters of the servant model, in turn, denounce the other four as being too introspective and churchy.

In passing one may note that the tensions here referred to are similar to those long recognized in comparative ecclesiology under rubrics such as priestly vs. prophetic, catholic vs. protestant, sacred vs. secular. But these dichotomies are too crude to do justice to the full spectrum of positions.

In any effort at evaluation we must beware of the tendency of each contestant to polemicize from a standpoint within his own preferred position. To make any real progress we must seek criteria that are acceptable to adherents of a number of different models. Seven such criteria (not all of them equally appealing to all members of all theological schools) come to mind:

1. *Basis in Scripture.* Nearly all Christians feel more comfortable if they can find a secure biblical basis for a doctrine they wish to defend—the clearer and more explicit the better.

2. *Basis in Christian tradition.* Not all Christians set the same value on tradition, but nearly all would agree that the testimony of Christian believers in the past in favor of a given doctrine is evidence in its favor. The more universal and constant the tradition the more convincing it is.

3. *Capacity to give Church members a sense of their corporate identity and mission.* Christian believers gener-

ally are convinced that they do have a special calling as Christians, and they turn to theology to clarify this. Theology has a practical function of supporting the Church in its faith and mission.

4. *Tendency to foster the virtues and values generally admired by Christians.* By their total upbringing Christians are inclined to prize faith, hope, disinterested love of God, sacrificial love of fellow men, honesty, humility, sorrow for sin, and the like. If they find that a doctrine or theological system sustains these values, they will be favorably inclined toward it; if it negates these values they will suspect that the idea is erroneous.

5. *Correspondence with the religious experience of men today.* In recent years there has been a revolt against making either the Bible or tradition a decisive norm apart from the experience of believers themselves. Granted the tremendous cultural shifts that have been taking place, it is to be expected that men today will approach the Christian message from a new point of view. Some models, much honored in the past, may prove to be excessively bound up with the concerns and dominant images of a culture not our own.

6. *Theological fruitfulness.* As noted in our first chapter, theological revolutions, like scientific revolutions, occur when the paradigms previously in use are found to be inadequate for the solution of present problems, and when better paradigms come into view. One criterion for the selection of new paradigms is their ability to solve problems that proved intractable by appeal to the older models, or to synthesize doctrines that previously appeared to be unrelated.

7. *Fruitfulness in enabling Church members to relate successfully to those outside their own group*—for example, to Christians of other traditions, to adherents of non-Christian religions, and to dedicated secular humanists.

To measure each of our five basic models by all seven of these criteria would at this point be wearisome. The indications already given in earlier chapters may be sufficient.

In a summary way, it may be proposed that the first criterion gives good support to the community and kerygmatic models; the second criterion, to the community model (though modern Roman Catholic tradition favors the institutional as well); the third criterion, to the institutional and kerygmatic models; the fourth criterion, to the sacramental and servant models; the fifth criterion, to the community and servant models; the sixth criterion, to the sacramental model, and the seventh criterion, to the community and servant models.

This variety of results makes it apparent that certain types of persons will be spontaneously drawn to certain models. Church officials have a tendency to prefer the institutional model; ecumenists, the community model; speculative theologians, the sacramental model; preachers and biblical scholars, the kerygmatic model; and secular activists, the servant model.

Are we then to conclude with an agreement to disagree —with a sterile repetition of the maxim, *"chaqu'un à son goût"*? This author's total life-experience prompts him to reject any such conclusion. He is convinced that to immure oneself behind a fixed theological position is humanly and spiritually disastrous. It is important at all costs to keep open the lines of communication between different theological schools and traditions.

Two general working principles may be invoked to support a reconciling approach. Neither of these principles is strictly demonstrable, but both of them seem to be favored by the accumulated experience of many good and wise persons. The first is that what any large group of Christian believers have confidently held over a considerable period of time should be accepted unless one has serious reasons for questioning it. Even if one comes to the conclusion that the tenet was false, one should at least make the effort to unveil the positive reason that made people accept error and thus to disclose the truth at the heart of the heresy.[2]

The second working principle is the view of John Stuart Mill, which commended itself to F. D. Maurice and

H. Richard Niebuhr, to the effect that men are more apt to be correct in what they affirm than in what they deny. "What we deny is generally something that lies outside our experience, and about which we can therefore say nothing."[3]

On the basis of these two principles, we must presume that the basic assertions implied in each of our five ecclesiological types are valid. Each of them in my opinion brings out certain important and necessary points. The institutional model makes it clear that the Church must be a structured community and that it must remain the kind of community Christ instituted. Such a community would have to include a pastoral office equipped with authority to preside over the worship of the community as such, to prescribe the limits of tolerable dissent, and to represent the community in an official way. The community model makes it evident that the Church must be united to God by grace, and that in the strength of that grace its members must be lovingly united to one another. The sacramental model brings home the idea that the Church must in its visible aspects—especially in its community prayer and worship—be a sign of the continuing vitality of the grace of Christ and of hope for the redemption that he promises. The kergymatic model accentuates the necessity for the Church to continue to herald the gospel and to move men to put their faith in Jesus as Lord and Savior. The diaconal model points up the urgency of making the Church contribute to the transformation of the secular life of man, and of impregnating human society as a whole with the values of the Kingdom of God.

On the other hand, it must be recognized that we cannot without qualification accept all five models, for they to some extent come into conflict with each other. They suggest different priorities and even lead to mutually antithetical assertions. Taken in isolation, each of the ecclesiological types could lead to serious imbalances and distortions. The institutional model, by itself, tends to become rigid, doctrinaire, and conformist; it could easily substitute the official Church for God, and this would be a form of idolatry. As a remedy, the structures of the Church must be seen as subordinate to its communal life and mission.

The second model, that of mystical communion, can arouse an unhealthy spirit of enthusiasm; in its search for religious experiences or warm, familial relationships, it could lead to false expectations and impossible demands, considering the vastness of the Church, the many goals for which it must labor, and its remoteness from its eschatological goal. As a remedy, one must call for patience, faith, and a concern for the greater and more universal good.

The third model, the sacramental, could lead to a sterile aestheticism and to an almost narcissistic self-contemplation. As a remedy, attention must be called to the values of structures, community, and mission brought out in the other models.

The fourth model, the kerygmatic, runs the risk of falling into the exaggerations of biblicist and fundamentalistic sects. It tends to oversimplify the process of salvation, to advertise "cheap grace," to be satisfied with words and professions rather than to insist on deeds, especially in the social and public arena. As a remedy, one must stress the necessity of incarnating one's faith in life and action.

The fifth model, the diaconal, could easily give the impression that man's final salvation is to be found within history, and could lure the Church into an uncritical acceptance of secular values, thus muting its distinctive witness to Christ and to its own heritage. As an antidote, one must insist on the provisional character of any good or evil experienced within history, and on the importance of looking always to Christ and to his Kingdom.

Granting the distinctive values of each of the five models and the undesirability of accepting any one model to the exclusion of the others, the question arises whether we ought not to look for some supermodel that combines the virtues of each of the five without suffering their limitations. Without asserting that the five models studied in this book are the only possible ones, I would be skeptical of the possibility of finding any one model that would be truly adequate; for the Church, as we have seen in Chapter I, is essentially a mystery. We are therefore condemned to work with models that are inadequate to the reality to which they point.

Our method must therefore be to harmonize the models in such a way that their differences become complementary rather than mutually repugnant. In order to do so, we shall have to criticize each of the models in the light of all the others. We must refrain from so affirming any one of the models as to deny, even implicitly, what the others affirm. In this way it may be possible to gain an understanding of the Church that transcends the limitations of any given model. We shall be able to qualify each of the models intrinsically in such a way as to introduce into it the values more expressly taught by the others. The models, as I understand them, are sufficiently flexible to be mutually open and compenetrable.

This being so, there is nothing to prevent a given theologian from building his own personal theology on one or another of the paradigms in the tradition. If one begins, for example, with the model of the Church as servant, one may then work backward and integrate into this model the values of the other four. One may say, for instance, that the Church serves mankind precisely by looking to Jesus, the Servant Lord, and by subjecting itself to the word of the gospel. Only by acknowledging the sovereignty of God's word can the Church avoid an uncritical and unhealthy complacency. The idea of the Church as servant of the gospel, moreover, may be said to imply that of the Church as sacrament, for it is precisely in serving that the Church most perfectly images forth the Son of Man, who came to serve and offer his life as a ransom for the many. A servant Church can effectively herald the gospel as a triumphal Church could not. Only in becoming a faithful servant of the Servant Lord can the Church effectively proclaim the good news of the Christian revelation. Thus the three models of servant, herald, and sacrament in many respects merge to make up a composite picture.

The coalescence, moreover, does not stop at this point.

It is precisely this servant Church that can best claim to be the Body of Christ—the same Body that in Jesus himself has been bruised for our sakes and made whole again by God. It is this servant Church, and no other, that can dare to claim that the Spirit of Christ really dwells in it. With its divine Lord this Church can say, "The Spirit of the Lord is upon me, because he has anointed me to preach good news to the poor. He has sent me to proclaim release to the captives and recovering of sight to the blind, to set at liberty those who are oppressed, to proclaim the acceptable year of the Lord" (Lk. 4:18–19). In this body the mutual hostilities of men are brought to an end and the members are united into a holy Temple in the Lord.

Within this servant Body, anointed by the Spirit of the Lord, there will be diversities of charism and service. There will be some who will be chosen by the Spirit and approved by the communities for offices of leadership. The flock of Christ will not be without pastors, committed to a life of dedicated service. There will be order and discipline, humility and obedience. In other words, there will be Church polity. Ecclesiastical office must seek to preserve the true spirit of the gospel and at the same time to adjust the Church to the needs of the times. There will be doctrine too, for the faith of the Church will be constantly nourished by the better formulation of that to which all are committed in Christ. The organization of the Church need not be pitted against its spirit and its life. According to the logic of the incarnation, the Church will seek always to strengthen its life by appropriate visible structures. The Church will not be an invisible "Kingdom of the Spirit," but a human institution, similar in many respects to other societies.

For blending the values in the various models, the sacramental type of ecclesiology in my opinion has special merit. It preserves the value of the institutional elements because the official structures of the Church give it clear and visible outlines, so that it can be a vivid sign. It preserves the community value, for if the Church were not a communion of love it could not be an authentic sign of

Christ. It preserves the dimension of proclamation, because only by reliance on Christ and by bearing witness to him, whether the message is welcomed or rejected, can the Church effectively point to Christ as the bearer of God's redemptive grace. This model, finally, preserves the dimension of worldly service, because without this the Church would not be a sign of Christ the servant.

One of the five models, I believe, cannot properly be taken as primary—and this is the institutional model. Of their very nature, I believe, institutions are subordinate to persons, structures are subordinate to life. "The sabbath was made for man, not man for the sabbath" (Mk. 2:27). Without calling into question the value and importance of institutions, one may feel that this value does not properly appear unless it can be seen that the structure effectively helps to make the Church a community of grace, a sacrament of Christ, a herald of salvation, and a servant of mankind.

In harmonizing the models, we should not behave as if we were trying to fit together the pieces of a difficult jigsaw puzzle. In a puzzle, one has no other data than the objective elements that have to be combined. In the field of theology the models must be seen against the horizon of the mysterious, nonobjective experience of grace from which they arose and by which they must, in turn, be revitalized. As we saw in our first chapter, only the grace experience, or, in other terminology, the inner enlightenment of the Holy Spirit, supplies man with the necessary tact and discretion so that he can see the values and limits of different models.

One final caution may be in order. Theologians often tend to assume that the essence of the Church somehow exists, like a dark continent, ready-made and awaiting only to be mapped. The Church, as a sociological entity, may be more correctly viewed as a "social construct."[4] In terms of sociological theory, one may say that the form of the Church is being constantly modified by the way in which the members of the Church externalize their own experience and in so doing transform the Church to which they already belong. Within the myriad possibilities left open by Scripture and tradition, the Church in every generation has to exercise options. It becomes what its leaders and its people choose to make of it. The fact that the Church of a certain century may have been primarily an institution does not prevent the Church in another generation from being more conspicuously a community of grace, a herald, a sacrament, or a servant.

The future forms of the Church lie beyond our power to foresee, except that we may be sure that they will be different from the forms of yesterday and today. The Church will not necessarily mirror the secular society of tomorrow, for it must avoid the kind of conformity with the world condemned by the Apostle (Rom. 12:2). On the other hand, the Church will have to make adjustments in order to survive in the society of the future and to confront the members of that society with the challenge of the gospel.

In view of the long-range changes going on in secular society and the impact they have been having on the Church in recent decades, it seems prudent to predict that the following five trends, already observable in recent Church history, will continue:[5]

1. *Modernization of structures.* The current structures of the Church, especially in Roman Catholicism, bear a very strong imprint of the past social structures of Western European society. In particular, the idea of an "unequal" society, in which certain members are set on a higher plane and made invulnerable to criticism and pressure from below, savors too much of earlier oligarchic regimes to be at home in the contemporary world. In its stead, modern society is adopting a more functional approach to authority. The task of Christianity will be to harmonize the right kind of functionalism and accountability with the evangelical idea of pastoral office as a representation of Christ's own authority. Here the Church, in my opinion, has an important contribution to make to the modern world. The traditional Christian conception

of authority as an exigent service remains valid and potentially fruitful.

2. *Ecumenical interplay.* The present denominational divisions among the Churches, in great part, no longer correspond with the real issues that respectively unite and divide Christians of our day. The debates that separated the churches in 1054 and 1520, while they may be revived in contemporary controversy, are no longer the really burning issues. Some method must be found to overcome these inherited divisions so that committed Christians in different denominational traditions may find each other once again in the same community of faith, dialogue, and worship. Short of full reunion there may be many possibilities of mutual recognition, doctrinal accord, joint worship, and practical cooperation.

3. *Internal pluralism.* Pluralism is already very great, perhaps too great, in some of the Protestant churches, but it has been slow to assert itself in Roman Catholicism. The strong centralization in modern Catholicism is due to historical accidents. It has been shaped in part by the homogeneous culture of medieval Europe and by the dominance of Rome, with its rich heritage of classical culture and legal organization. In the Counter Reformation this uniformity was increased by an almost military posture of resistance to the inroads of alien systems of thought such as Protestantism and deistic rationalism. The decentralization of the future will involve a certain measure of de-Romanization. There is little reason today why Roman law, the Roman language, Roman conceptual schemes, and Roman liturgical forms should continue to be normative for the worldwide Church. With increasing decentralization, the Catholic Church in various regions will be able to enter more vitally into the life of different peoples and to relate itself more positively to the traditions of other Christian denominations.

4. *Provisionality.* In a world of increasing "rapidation" and "future shock" the Church must continue to provide a zone of relative stability and to enable the faithful to relate meaningfully to their religious past. But the Church

must not allow itself to become a mere relic or museum piece. It must prove capable of responding creatively to the demands of new situations and to the needs of generations yet to come. Church decisions will increasingly take on the form not of immutable decrees but of tentative measures taken in view of passing needs and temporary opportunities.

5. *Voluntariness*. In the "post-Constantinian" or "diaspora" situation of our day, the Church will not be able to rely to the same extent as formerly on canonical penalties and sociological pressures in order to keep its members in line. Anyone at any time will be able to opt out of the Church without fearing legal or social sanctions. Furthermore, the internal pluralism of the Church itself will be such that directives from on high will be variously applied in different regions, so that the top officers will not be able to control in detail what goes on at the local level.

In this situation the Church will have to rule more by persuasion and less by force. The officers will have to obtain a good measure of consensus behind their decisions, and this in turn will require increased dialogue. To some extent this development may seem a humiliation for the Church, but in another sense it may appear as progress. The Church will be better able to appear as a home of freedom and as "a sign and a safeguard of the transcendence of the human person."[6]

All these predictions seem to be solidly based on the major social trends of recent centuries. If the Church is to carry out its mission effectively, it must take cognizance of these social movements. But will it in fact enter vigorously into dialogue with the new world that is being born before our eyes, or will it on the contrary become more than ever a vestige of the past? In principle it would be possible for the Church to refuse to adapt itself as the times require, and thus to become an ossified remnant of its former self. Such a Church would no doubt continue to exist thanks to the richness of its heritage, but it would no longer be the home of living faith and prophetic commitment.[7]

Because the Church carries with it so large a heritage from the past, there is a constant temptation for its members to cling to the ways of their ancestors and to resist the call to confront the world of today. In the wake of Vatican II, with its large promises of renewal and reform, we are presently witnessing a new surge of legalism and reaction. The staying power of the conservatives, and their determination to adhere to ancient forms, have surpassed the expectations of starry-eyed reformers who expected to have an easy time of it after the last Council. Will static traditionalism have the last word? Or will churchmen of prophetic vision arise to lead the People of God resolutely into the future?

What the Church is to become depends to a great degree on the responsiveness of men, but even more importantly, it depends on the free initiatives of the Holy Spirit. If man is free and dynamic, the Spirit of God is even more so. To carry out their mission in the Church, Christians must therefore open their ears and hear "what the Spirit says to the churches" (Apoc. 2:17). It is not enough for them to listen to the Church unless the Church, through its responsible leaders, is listening to the Spirit. The Spirit alone can give the necessary judgment and discretion. "The spiritual man judges all things, but is himself judged by no one" (1 Cor. 2:15).

Like the Israelites of old, many Christians today are saying, "Our bones are dried up, our hope is lost, we are clean cut off" (Ezek. 37:11). The Lord must say to us, as he did to Ezekiel, "Behold, I will open your graves, and raise you from your graves, O my people" (v. 13). If life is to be breathed into those dead bones of doctrinal, ritual, and hierarchical organization that, in the eyes of many viewers, now constitute the Church, the Spirit of the Lord must send prophets to his people. The charismatic movement of the past few years gives signs, not wholly unambiguous, that the Holy Spirit may be answering the longings of men's hearts.

Under the leading of the Holy Spirit the images and forms of Christian life will continue to change, as they have in previous centuries.[8] In a healthy community of faith the production of new myths and symbols goes on apace. The ecclesiologists of the future will no doubt devise new models for thinking about the Church. But what is new in Christianity always grows out of the past and has its roots in Scripture and tradition. On the basis of the relative continuity of the past two thousand years it seems safe to predict that the analogues and paradigms discussed in this book will retain their significance for ecclesiology through many generations yet to come.

# Notes

## CHAPTER I

1. *De controversiis*, tom. 2, liber 3, *De ecclesia militante*, cap. 2, "De definitione Ecclesiae" (Naples: Giuliano, 1857), vol. 2, p. 75.

2. Jérôme Hamer, *The Church Is a Communion* (New York: Sheed & Ward, 1964), p. 84.

3. On the notion of mystery in the Bible see especially R. E. Brown, "The Semitic Background of the New Testament *Mysterion*," *Biblica* 39 (1958), 426–48; 40 (1959), 70–87. On the use of the term "mystery" in dogmatic theology see K. Rahner, "The Concept of Mystery in Catholic Theology," *Theological Investigations* 4 (Baltimore: Helicon, 1966), pp. 36–73. Further bibliography is in R. E. Brown, "Mystery (in the Bible)," *New Catholic Encyclopedia* 10 (New York: McGraw-Hill, 1967), pp. 148–51; A. Dulles, "Mystery (in Theology)," ibid., pp. 151–53.

4. Thomas Aquinas, *Summa theologiae*, 2a2ae, q. 1, art. 4, ad 3; qu. 45, art. 2, *in corp*.

5. Quoted in H. Küng, Y. Congar, and D. O'Hanlon (eds.), *Council Speeches of Vatican II* (Glen Rock, N.J.: Paulist Press, 1964), p. 26.

6. See on this subject I. T. Ramsey, *Religious Language* (New York: Macmillan Paperbacks, 1963); I. T. Ramsey, *Models and Mystery* (New York: Oxford University Press, 1964); Max Black, *Models and Metaphors* (Ithaca: Cornell University Press, 1962).

7. G. Weigel, "How Is the Council Going?," *America* 109 (December 7, 1963), 730.

8. *Council Speeches*, op. cit., p. 25.

9. Philadelphia: Westminster, 1960.

10. Cf. Y. Congar, *L'Eglise de S. Augustin à l'époque moderne* (Paris: Cerf, 1970), p. 44.

11. On the theology of symbol see F. W. Dillistone (ed.), *Myth and Symbol* (London: SPCK, 1966); Thomas Fawcett, *The Symbolic Language of Religion* (London: SCM, 1970), and Karl Rahner, "The Theology of Symbol," *Theological Investigations* 4, op. cit., pp. 221–52. Further bibliography is in A. Dulles, "Symbol in Revelation," *New Catholic Encyclopedia*, Vol. 13, pp. 861–63.

12. On the sociological function of images and symbols see Kenneth E. Boulding, *The Image* (Ann Arbor: University of Michigan, 1956) and Robert N. Bellah, "Transcendence in Contemporary Piety," *Beyond Belief* (New York: Harper & Row, 1970), pp. 196–208.

13. P. Minear, *Images of the Church in the New Testament* (Philadelphia: Westminster Press, 1960), p. 24.

14. I. T. Ramsey, *Models and Mystery*, p. 14.

15. E. Cousins, "Models and the Future of Theology," *Continuum* 7 (1969), 78–91. On models in theology see also John McIntyre, *The Shape of Christology* (London: SCM, 1966), pp. 54–81, and B. Lonergan, *Method in Theology* (New York: Herder & Herder, 1972), pp. 284–85.

16. John Powell, *The Mystery of the Church* (Milwaukee: Bruce, 1967), p. 8.

17. *Ecclesiam suam*, No. 39 (Glen Rock, N.J.: Paulist Press, 1964), p. 31.

18. T. S. Kuhn, *The Structure of Scientific Revolutions*, (2nd ed., enlarged (Chicago: University of Chicago Press, 1970), p. 175.

19. *Mystici Corporis*, 3rd ed., No. 17 (New York: America Press, 1957) Tromp ed. (3rd ed., Rome: Gregory University, 1958), No. 13.

20. Minear, op. cit., p. 253.


# CHAPTER II

1. *De controversiis*, tom. 2, lib. 3, cap. 2 (Naples: Giuliano, 1857), vol. 2, p. 75.

2. B. C. Butler, *The Idea of the Church* (Baltimore: Helicon, 1962), p. 39.

3. Y. Congar, *Lay People in the Church* (Westminster, Md.: Newman, 1965), p. 45.

4. The *primum schema* or first draft of the Constitution on the Church is in *Collectio Lacensis* (Freiburg: Herder, 1890), Vol. 7, pp. 567–78. It is here quoted from the translation in J. Neuner and H. Roos, *The Teaching of the Catholic Church* (Staten Island, N.Y.: Alba House, 1967), No. 361, pp. 213–14. This work will henceforth be abbreviated NR.

5. "For St Irenaeus, the *charisma veritatis* is not a power by which the hierarchy defines doctrine, it is the doctrine itself, the precious spiritual gift entrusted to the Church," Y. Congar, *Tradition and Traditions* (New York: Macmillan, 1967), p. 177.

6. NR, 369. This notion of the "unequal society" is even more strongly put by Pius X in *Vehementer nos, Acta Sanctae Sedis* 39 (1906–7), pp. 8–9.

7. The text of this speech is in *Acta Concilii Vaticani II*, Vol.

1, Part 4 (Vatican City: Typis Polyglottis, 1971), pp. 142–44.

8. H. Denzinger and A. Schönmetzer, *Enchiridion symbolorum,* 32nd ed. (Freiburg: Herder, 1963) [hereafter abbreviated *DS*], Nos. 1601 and 1775; *NR*, 413 and 637.

9. *DS*, 3058; *NR*, 377.

10. Even the Marian dogmas of the Immaculate Conception and the Assumption are asserted to have been revealed by God (*DS*, 3803, 3903; *NR*, 325, 334c). This has to be reconciled with the assertion that revelation was complete with the apostles (*DS*, 3421).

11. This method is particularly associated with the name of Ambroise Gardeil, O.P. (1859–1931), who expounded it in the *Revue thomiste* for 1903. See Yves Congar, *A History of Theology* (Garden City, N.Y.: Doubleday, 1968), pp. 236–37.

12. Pius XII, *Humani generis* (1950), No. 36; *DS*, 3886, with reference to Pius IX, *Inter gravissimas*, 1870.

13. *Mystici Corporis*, America Press ed., No. 29; Tromp ed., No. 21.

14. *De ecclesiae unitate* 6; ed. G. Hartel, CSEL III/1 (Vienna: 1868), p. 214.

15. Vatican I schema, Chap. 7; *NR*, 365.

16. Without repudiating this concept of Catholic Action, Vatican II taught that the laity have an apostolic calling proper to them by virtue of their baptism and confirmation. See Decree on the Apostolate of the Laity, Art. 20 (with official footnotes referring to Pius XI and Pius XII).

17. For a fuller explanation of the points raised in this paragraph see Thomas Luckmann, *The Invisible Religion* (New York: Macmillan, 1967); Michael Novak, *Ascent of the Mountain, Flight of the Dove* (New York: Harper & Row, 1970), Chap. 5; Gregory Baum, *New Horizon* (New York: Paulist Press, 1972), pp. 133–36.

## CHAPTER III

1. This antithesis owes its popularity to Ferdinand Tönnies, who in 1887 published his classic work, *Gemeinschaft und Gesellschaft* (English translation, *Community and Society*, New York: Harper Torchbooks, 1963).

2. Charles H. Cooley, *Social Organization* (1909; reprinted New York: Schocken Books, 1967), pp. 23–31.

3. C. H. Cooley, R. C. Angell, and L. J. Carr, *Introductory Sociology* (New York: Charles Scribner's Sons, 1933), pp. 55–56; cf. John C. McKinney, introduction to Tönnies, op. cit., pp. 14–15.

4. Ibid.

5. Such is the view of Rudolph Sohm, as summarized and ac-

cepted by Emil Brunner, *The Misunderstanding of the Church* (London: Lutterworth, 1952), p. 107.

6. Ibid., p. 17.

7. D. Bonhoeffer, *The Communion of Saints* (New York: Harper & Row, 1963), p. 123. On this subject William Kuhns comments:

"Bonhoeffer's thinking on the Church as community has not received the attention it deserves. The failure is deeply unfortunate, because Bonhoeffer's identification of the Church with personal community is surely as revolutionary as his later definition of the Church in terms of its going out to the world. . . .

"The implications for Catholics of Bonhoeffer's thought on community should be immediately noticeable. It is easy to see why *Life Together* would be more popular among Catholics (especially religious) than among Protestants; Catholics have shown a greater fascination, a more profound interest in the meaning of community as a mandate of Christ. Yet what makes Bonhoeffer's thought on community so relevant and significant to Catholics is the fact that no Catholic theologian has cut to the central issue of identifying the Church *as* community so consciously as Bonhoeffer has." *In Pursuit of Dietrich Bonhoeffer* (Dayton, O.: Pflaum, 1967), p. 253.

8. Augsburg: Haas und Grabherr, 1931. For a more recent variant on this position see Werner Stark, *The Sociology of Religion*, 5 vols., 1966–72 (New York: Fordham University Press). Stark comments on Rademacher in Vol. 5, pp. 72–75.

9. These ideas are clearly set forth in Congar's *Lay People in the Church* (Westminster, Md.: Newman, 1965), pp. 28–58.

10. J. Hamer, *The Church Is a Communion* (New York: Sheed & Ward, 1964), p. 93.

11. Ibid., pp. 159–64, 204.

12. For bibliography on the Pauline concept of the Church as body of Christ see H. Küng, *The Church* (New York: Sheed & Ward, 1968), p. 225. Küng's own treatment of this exegetical question is on pp. 228–34.

13. Stanislaus J. Grabowski, *The Church: An Introduction to the Theology of St. Augustine* (St. Louis: Herder, 1957), pp. 3–92.

14. Thomas Aquinas' notion of the Church as a communion of grace is presented by Y. Congar, *The Mystery of the Church* (Baltimore: Helicon, 1960), pp. 97–117; *L'Eglise de S. Augustin à l'époque moderne* (Paris: Cerf, 1970), pp. 232–40.

15. E. Mersch, *The Whole Christ* (Milwaukee: Bruce, 1938); *The Theology of the Mystical Body* (St. Louis: Herder, 1958).

16. For the antecedents of the encyclical *Mystici Corporis* see Hamer, op. cit., pp. 18–20; also F. Malmberg, *Ein Leib, ein Geist* (Freiburg: Herder, 1960), pp. 24–38.

17. America Press ed., Nos. 21–23; Tromp ed., No. 17.

18. Arts. 8–9.

19. See below, Chaps. VIII and IX.

20. *Lumen gentium*, Art. 9.

21. *Lumen gentium*, Art. 8; *Unitatis redintegratio*, Arts. 4 and 6.

22. "The Church: People of God," *Concilium* 1 (Glen Rock, N.J.: Paulist Press, 1965), 11–37.

23. Especially *Una Persona mystica*, 3rd ed. (Paderborn: Schöningh, 1968). For a summary in English of some of Mühlen's leading ideas, see Sabbas J. Kilian, "The Holy Spirit in Christ and Christians," *American Benedictine Review* 20 (1969), 99–121.

24. See, for instance, Max Delespesse, *The Church Community: Leaven and Life Style* (Ottawa, Ont., Canada: Catholic Centre of St. Paul University, 1969); also Stephen B. Clark, *Building Christian Communities* (Notre Dame, Ind.: Ave Maria Press, 1972).

25. *Against Heresies*, 3, 24, 1 (*PG* 7, 966).

26. See L. Hertling, *Communio: Church and Papacy in Early Christianity* (Chicago: Loyola University Press, 1972).

27. Paul Tillich, *Systematic Theology*, Vol. 3 (Chicago: University of Chicago Press, 1963), pp. 162–72. Cf. below, Chap. IX, note 9.

28. Thus one may question the universal validity of Rademacher's statement: "The more intimate man's relationship to God is, the warmer also will be the relationship of men to one another," *Die Kirche als Gemeinschaft und Gesellschaft* (Augsburg: Haas und Grabherr, 1931), p. 48.

29. G. Baum, *New Horizon* (New York: Paulist Press, 1972), pp. 141–42.

## CHAPTER IV

1. For an exposition with ample references to the ancient and modern theologians, see P. Smulders, "L'Eglise sacrement du salut," in G. Baraúna (ed.), *L'Eglise de Vatican II* (Paris: Cerf, 1967), Vol. 2, pp. 313–38. On Augustine in particular see Y. Congar, "Introduction générale," *Oeuvres de St. Augustin*, Vol. 28, *Traités Anti-Donatistes* (Bruges: Desclée de Brouwer, 1963), pp. 86–115. On Aquinas see Y. Congar, *The Mystery of the Church* (Baltimore: Helicon, 1960), Chap. 3, esp. pp. 113–16.

2. H. de Lubac, *Catholicism* (London: Burns, Oates, and Washbourne, 1950), p. 29.

3. Ibid., p. 35.

4. "Membership of the Church," *Theological Investigations*, Vol. 2 (Baltimore: Helicon, 1963), pp. 1–88; "The Church and the Sacraments," *Inquiries* (New York: Herder & Herder, 1964), pp. 191–257.

5. O. Semmelroth, *Die Kirche als Ursakrament* (Frankfurt: Knecht, 1953).

6. E. Schillebeeckx, *Christ the Sacrament of the Encounter with*

*God* (New York: Sheed & Ward, 1963), esp. Chap. 2, "The Church, Sacrament of the Risen Christ," pp. 47–89.

7. P. Smulders, loc. cit. (note 1).

8. Y. Congar, *The Church That I Love* (Denville, N.J.: Dimension Books, 1969), Chap. 2, "The Church, Universal Sacrament of Salvation."

9. J. Groot, "The Church as Sacrament of the World," *Concilium*, Vol. 31 (New York: Paulist Press, 1968), pp. 51–66.

10. G. Martelet, "De la sacramentalité propre à l'Eglise," *Nouvelle revue théologique* 95 (1973), 25–42.

11. The official text of this letter was apparently never published. An excerpt, reprinted from an unofficial version in the *American Ecclesiastical Review* for 1952, may be found in DS 3866–73.

12. For example, *Lumen gentium*, Arts. 9 and 48; *Sacrosanctum concilium*, Art. 26 (quoting Cyprian); *Ad gentes*, Art. 5, and *Gaudium et spes*, Art. 42.

13. *Sacrosanctum concilium*, Art. 10.

14. Ibid., Art. 41.

15. Cf. Karl Rahner, *Spirit in the World* (New York: Herder & Herder, 1968).

16. K. Rahner, "Penance," *Sacramentum Mundi* 4 (New York: Herder & Herder, 1969), pp. 385–99.

17. *NR*, 486; *DS*, 1639.

18. "If any one shall say that the sacraments of the New Law do not contain the grace which they signify, or that they do not confer that grace on those who place no obstacles in its way . . . *anathema sit*." *NR*, 418; *DS*, 1606.

19. See the article "Jesus Christ" in *Sacramentum Mundi*, Vol. 3 (New York: Herder & Herder, 1969), pp. 191–92 (Grillmeier), and pp. 197–98, 204–5 (Rahner).

20. *The Church and the Sacraments*, p. 317.

21. Quesnel was condemned in 1713 for teaching that "outside the Church no grace is granted," *DS*, 2429.

22. *The Church Is a Communion*, pp. 87–91.

23. *Church: The Continuing Quest* (Paramus, N.J.: Newman Press, 1970), p. 61.

24. *The Uppsala Report* (Geneva: World Council of Churches, 1968), p. 17.


# CHAPTER V

1. R. P. McBrien, *Church: The Continuing Quest* (New York: Newman, 1970), p. 11.

2. K. Barth, *Church Dogmatics* I/1 (Edinburgh: T. and T. Clark, 1936), pp. 298–300.

3. Ibid., pp. 15, 190, 204.

4. Ibid., pp. 126, 301.

5. K. Barth, *Dogmatics in Outline* (New York: Harper Torch-books, 1959), pp. 142–43.

6. K. Barth's Amsterdam address, published in *The Universal Church in God's Design* (Vol. 1 of *Man's Disorder and God's Design*, New York: Harper & Brothers, 1949), p. 68.

7. H. Küng, *The Church* (New York: Sheed & Ward, 1968), pp. 79–104.

8. Ibid., p. 84.

9. Ibid., p. 92.

10. Ibid., p. 96.

11. R. Bultmann, *Theology of the New Testament*, Vol. 1 (New York: Scribner's, 1951), pp. 306–14.

12. H. W. Bartsch (ed.), *Kerygma and Myth*, Vol. 1 (New York: Harper Torchbooks, 1961), pp. 209–10. The same passage is repeated in Bultmann's *Jesus Christ and Mythology* (London: SCM, 1958), pp. 82–83.

13. E. Fuchs, *Studies of the Historical Jesus* (Studies in Biblical Theology, 42) (London: SCM, 1964), pp. 208–9.

14. James M. Robinson, "Hermeneutic Since Barth," *The New Hermeneutic* (New York: Harper & Row, 1964), p. 58.

15. G. Ebeling, *The Nature of Faith* (Philadelphia: Fortress Press, 1961), pp. 146–47.

16. Chapter 4, note 1.

17. L. Newbigin, *The Household of God* (London: SCM, 1953), pp. 49–59.

18. Ibid., p. 82.

19. *Sacrosanctum concilium*, Art. 7.

20. *Dei verbum*, Art. 1.

21. *Dei verbum*, Art. 10.

22. *Unitatis redintegratio*, Art. 21.

23. Karl Barth, *Ad Limina Apostolorum* (Richmond: John Knox Press, 1968), p. 27.

24. R. P. McBrien, *Church: The Continuing Quest*, p. 58.

## CHAPTER VI

1. *DS*, 2980.

2. See E. E. Y. Hales, *Pope John and His Revolution* (Garden City, N.Y.: Doubleday, 1965), pp. 33–34. The Knox translation of "Darkness over the Earth" is here used.

3. Quoted in W. M. Abbott (ed.), *The Documents of Vatican II* (New York: America Press, 1966), p. 704.

4. Ibid., p. 706.

5. Ibid., p. 712.

6. *Gaudium et spes*, Art. 59.

7. Ibid., Art. 44.

8. Ibid., Art. 62.

9. On this method see R. P. McBrien, *Church: The Continuing*

*Quest,* pp. 12–21; A. Dulles, "The Church Is Communications," *Catholic Mind* 69 (October 1971), 6–16.

10. Richard Cardinal Cushing, *The Servant Church* (Boston: Daughters of St. Paul), p. 6.

11. Ibid., pp. 7, 8.

12. Unpublished manuscript, "Comment je vois," quoted by E. Rideau, *The Thought of Teilhard de Chardin* (New York: Harper & Row, 1967), p. 597.

13. P. Teilhard de Chardin, *The Divine Milieu* (New York: Harper & Brothers, 1960), p. 138.

14. D. Bonhoeffer, *Ethics* (New York: Macmillan Paperbacks, 1965), p. 350.

15. D. Bonhoeffer, *Letters and Papers from Prison,* rev. ed. (New York: Macmillan, 1967), pp. 203–4.

16. G. Winter, *The New Creation as Metropolis* (New York: Macmillan, 1963), p. 55.

17. Ibid., p. 72.

18. H. Cox, *The Secular City* (New York: Macmillan, 1965), p. 134.

19. J. A. T. Robinson, *The New Reformation?* (Philadelphia: Westminster Press, 1965), p. 92.

20. R. Adolfs, *The Grave of God: Has the Church a Future?* (London: Burns & Oates, 1967), pp. 109–17.

21. E. Bianchi, *Reconciliation: The Function of the Church* (New York: Sheed & Ward, 1969), pp. x and 168.

22. R. P. McBrien, *Do We Need the Church?* (New York: Harper & Row, 1969), pp. 98–99.

23. Ibid., p. 229; cf. *Church: The Continuing Quest,* p. 85.

24. Cf. H. W. Beyer, "Diakoneō, etc." in G. Kittel, *Theological Dictionary of the New Testament,* Vol. 2 (Grand Rapids, Mich.: Eerdmans, 1964), pp. 81–93.

25. See above, Chap. 5, note 24.

26. G. C. C. O'Collins, "Notes and Comments: On R. P. McBrien's *Do We Need the Church?,*" *Heythrop Journal* 10 (1969), 416–19.

27. Y. Congar, *Power and Poverty in the Church* (Baltimore: Helicon, 1964), p. 65.

## CHAPTER VII

1. "The Church and the Parousia of Christ," *Theological Investigations,* Vol. 6 (Baltimore: Helicon, 1969), p. 298.

2. R. P. McBrien, *Do We Need the Church?* (New York: Harper & Row, 1969), p. 98.

3. H. Küng, *The Church,* pp. 92–93.

4. *Theology and the Kingdom of God* (Philadelphia: Westminster, 1969), pp. 76–77.

5. For a fuller development of the biblical and historical evi-

dences for my position see A. Dulles, "The Church as Eschatological Community," to be published in J. Papin (ed.), *The Eschaton: A Community of Love* (Villanova, Pa.: Villanova University Press, 1973).

6. Riesenfeld's unpublished lecture on this subject is summarized by Benedikt Schwank, "Daniel—Jesus—Paulus," *Erbe und Auftrag* 47 (1971), 506–8.

7. *Lumen gentium*, Art. 48.

8. R. P. McBrien, *Church: The Continuing Quest*, pp. 14–21.

9. *Die Predigt Jesu vom Reiche Gottes*, 2nd ed., p. 145; quoted by J. Moltmann, *Theology of Hope* (London: SCM, 1967), p. 38.

10. Moltmann, ibid., pp. 38–39.

11. Werner's classic work, *Die Entstehung des christlichen Dogmas, problemgeschichtlich dargestellt*, 1941, is discussed by O. Cullmann, especially in his *Salvation in History* (New York: Harper & Row, 1967), pp. 37–42.

12. Rosemary R. Ruether, "An Invitation to Jewish-Christian Dialogue: In What Sense Can We Say That Jesus Was 'The Christ'?," *The Ecumenist* 10 (1972), 17–24. This article will be the conclusion of Mrs. Ruether's forthcoming book, *Messiah of Israel and the Cosmic Christ*.

13. C. H. Dodd, *The Apostolic Preaching and Its Developments* (London: Hodder & Stoughton, 1936), p. 93.

14. Ibid., p. 96.

15. C. H. Dodd, *The Interpretation of the Fourth Gospel* (Cambridge: University Press, 1958), p. 447, note 1. See also Dodd's *The Coming of Christ* (Cambridge: Cambridge University Press, 1954).

16. See R. P. McBrien, *The Church in the Thought of Bishop John Robinson* (Philadelphia: Westminster Press, 1966), pp. 44–73.

17. W. A. Visser 't Hooft (ed.), *The New Delhi Report: The Third Assembly of the World Council of Churches* (London: SCM, 1962), p. 90.

18. *Lumen gentium*, Art. 8. The same metaphor of pilgrimage reappears in *Unitatis redintegratio*, Art. 3.

19. *Dei verbum*, Art. 8.

20. *Sacrosanctum concilium*, Art. 2.

21. R. Laurentin, *Liberation, Development, and Salvation* (Maryknoll: Orbis, 1972), pp. 54–60.

22. Cf. *Sacrosanctum concilium*, Arts. 2 and 41.

23. O. Cullmann, *Christ and Time* (Philadelphia: Westminster, 1950), pp. 160–62. See also his "Eschatology and Missions in the New Testament," in G. H. Anderson (ed.), *The Theology of the Christian Mission* (New York: McGraw-Hill, 1961), pp. 42–54.

24. *Ad gentes*, Art. 9, with footnotes.

25. Thomas Aquinas, *Summa theol.*, 1a2ae, q. 106, Art. 4, ad 4.

26. W. Pannenberg, *Theology and the Kingdom of God*, p. 75.

27. Ibid., p. 74.

28. J. Moltmann, *Theology of Hope*, pp. 327–28.

29. E. Schillebeeckx, *God the Future of Man* (New York: Sheed & Ward, 1968), Chaps. 5–6.

30. J. B. Metz, *Theology of the World* (New York: Herder & Herder, paperback, 1971), p. 116, italics in original.

31. K. Rahner, "Christianity and the 'New Man,'" *Theological Investigations*, Vol. 5, p. 149.

## CHAPTER VIII

1. For the history of the apologetical and theological usage of the four notes, see Y. Congar, *L'Eglise une, sainte, catholique, et apostolique* (Paris: Cerf, 1970). H. Küng also gives many valuable materials in his *The Church*, Part D, pp. 263–359.

2. Pierre Nautin, *Je crois à l'Esprit saint dans la sainte Eglise pour la résurrection de la chair* (Paris: Cerf, 1947).

3. *Lumen gentium*, Art. 8.

4. Yves de la Brière, "Eglise (Question des Notes)," *Dictionnaire apologétique de la foi catholique*, Vol. 1 (Paris: Beauchesne, 1925), col. 1284.

5. Gustave Thils, *Les notes de l'Eglise dans l'apologétique catholique depuis la Réforme* (Gembloux: Duculot, 1937), p. 197.

6. DS, 2888; NR, 354.

7. Thils, op. cit., p. 136.

8. G. Weigel, "Summula Ecclesiologica" (multilithed notes for students) (Woodstock, Md., 1954), p. 78.

9. Thils, op. cit., pp. 275–85.

10. For an example of this approach see J. L. Witte, "One, Holy, Catholic, and Apostolic," in H. Vorgrimler (ed.), *One, Holy, Catholic, and Apostolic* (London: Sheed & Ward, 1968), pp. 3–43. Witte's approach here is in its main lines similar to that of Congar in the work cited in note 1 above.

11. DS, 3013; NR, 356.

12. René Latourelle, *Christ and the Church: Signs of Salvation* (Staten Island, N.Y.: Alba House, 1972), pp. 113–14.

13. *Lumen gentium*, Art. 13.

14. Cf. Stephen Laszlo, "Sin in the Holy Church of God," in H. Küng and others, *Council Speeches of Vatican II*, pp. 44–48.

15. The idea of the "sinful Church" is accepted by Rahner and Küng, but is rejected by C. Journet on the ground that, although there is sin in the Church, the Church itself is not sinful, for the sinner in sinning to that extent separates himself from the Church. Any theologian's answer to this disputed question will depend very much on the ecclesiological models from which he works.

16. *Lumen gentium*, Art. 15.

17. *Gaudium et spes*, Art. 19; cf. Art. 43.

18. *Unitatis redintegratio*, Art. 16.

19. W. Pannenberg, "The Significance of Eschatology for the Understanding of the Apostolicity and Catholicity of the Church," *One in Christ* 6 (1970), 429.

20. Adding emphasis to this position, the Congregation of the Doctrine of the Faith, in a Declaration of June 24, 1973, stated that Catholics are not free "to hold that Christ's Church nowhere really exists today and that it is to be considered only as an end which all Churches and ecclesial communities must strive to reach." *Mysterium Ecclesiae* (Washington, D.C.: USCC, 1973), p. 3.

## CHAPTER IX

1. The reason for this change of wording was ecumenical. According to the *relator* at the Council, "subsists in" was substituted for "is" "so that the expression may harmonize better with the affirmation [in this same paragraph of the Constitution] concerning the ecclesial elements that are present elsewhere."

2. *Mystici Corporis*, America Press ed., Art. 29; Tromp ed., Art. 21.

3. *Humani generis*, Art. 44, H. Denzinger and C. Bannwart, *Enchiridion symbolorum*, 30 ed. (Freiburg: Herder, 1955), No. 2319.

4. Pius XI, Encyclical Letter *Mortalium animos* (January 6, 1928), in G. K. A. Bell (ed.), *Documents on Christian Unity*, 2nd ser. (London: Oxford University Press, 1930), p. 61.

5. *DS*, 2888.

6. Lukas Vischer (ed.), *A Documentary History of the Faith and Order Movement 1927–1963* (St. Louis: Bethany Press, 1963), p. 174.

7. *Unitatis redintegratio*, Art. 3.

8. This is the view expressed by Congar in various places; e.g., *Dialogue Between Christians* (Westminster, Md.: Newman, 1966), pp. 184–213.

9. Paul Tillich, *Systematic Theology*, Vol. 3 (Chicago: University of Chicago Press, 1963), pp. 162–72.

10. *Mystici Corporis*, America Press ed., Art. 79; Tromp ed., Art. 63.

11. Ibid., America Press ed., Art. 69; Tromp ed., Art. 55.

12. The text of Cardinal Lercaro's speech is given in *The Ecumenist* 2 (1964), 90.

13. *Lumen gentium*, Art. 8.

14. "The Ecclesial Reality of Other Churches," *Concilium* 4 (Glen Rock, N.J.: Paulist Press, 1965), 82.

15. At Uppsala in 1968 the Assembly Committee on Faith and Order shrewdly commented: "We welcome . . . the statement of the Faith and Order Commission that its task remains 'to proclaim

the oneness of the Church of Christ' and to keep before the Council and the churches 'the obligation to manifest that unity for the sake of the Lord and for the better accomplishment of his mission in the world.' However, it may be asked whether the problem of unity can be reduced simply to the increase in 'manifestation,' or whether there is an internal break of unity which needs to be recovered. The restoration and fulfillment of the unity of the churches is the most urgent task to which Faith and Order has to call them." *The Uppsala Report* (Geneva: World Council of Churches, 1968), pp. 223–24.

16. Karl Rahner, *The Dynamic Element in the Church* (New York: Herder & Herder, 1964), p. 63.

17. J. Gribomont, "Du sacrement de l'Eglise et de ses réalisations imparfaites," *Irénikon* 22 (1949), 345–67, quotation from p. 362.

18. H. Küng, *The Church* (New York: Sheed & Ward, 1968), p. 282.

19. K. Barth, *Church Dogmatics* IV/1 (New York: Scribner's, 1956), p. 684.

20. *Unitatis redintegratio,* Art. 12.

21. *Ad gentes,* Art. 15.

22. Robert McAfee Brown, *The Ecumenical Revolution,* rev. ed. (Garden City, N.Y.: Doubleday, 1969), pp. 407–8.

23. Lewis S. Mudge, *The Crumbling Walls* (Philadelphia: Westminster Press, 1970), pp. 88–89.

24. *Method in Theology,* p. 362.

25. Ibid., p. 368.

26. Report of the Section on Service, in W. A. Visser 't Hooft (ed.), *The New Delhi Report,* 93–94.

27. *The Uppsala Report,* No. 21, p. 18.

28. Text in Oliver S. Tomkins (ed.), *The Third World Conference on Faith and Order* (London: SCM, 1953), p. 151.

29. Thomas Sartory, *The Oecumenical Movement and the Unity of the Church* (Westminster, Md.: Newman, 1963), pp. 60 and 136.

30. H. Küng, *The Church,* p. 281.

31. W. A. Visser 't Hooft (ed.), *The Evanston Report: The Second Assembly of the World Council of Churches, 1954* (London: SCM, 1955), p. 94. This statement by the Orthodox delegation at Evanston agrees well with the recent statement of the Congregation of the Doctrine of the Faith, quoted in our Chapter VIII, note 20.

32. *Unitatis redintegratio,* Art. 24.

33. *Una mystica Persona,* pp. 543–44.

34. W. Kasper, "Der ekklesiologische Charakter der nichtkatholischen Kirchen," *Theologische Quartalschrift* 145 (1965), 62.

## CHAPTER X

1. B. Dupuy, "Is There a Dogmatic Distinction between the Function of Priests and the Function of Bishops?," *Concilium* 34 (Glen Rock, N.J.: Paulist Press, 1968), pp. 74–86. Dupuy accepts the opinion of A. Duval that Trent did not intend to give dogmatic status to the distinctions among bishops, presbyters, and ministers, although *DS*, 966 has often been read as though it meant to affirm this.

2. *Lumen gentium*, Art. 18.

3. *Presbyterorum ordinis*, Art. 6.

4. Yves Congar, "My Pathfindings in the Theology of Laity and Ministries," *The Jurist* 32 (1972), 169–88.

5. T. F. O'Meara, "Towards a Roman Catholic Theology of the Presbytery," *Heythrop Journal* 10 (1969), 390–404, quotation from p. 401.

6. H. Küng, *Why Priests?* (Garden City, N.Y.: Doubleday, 1972), pp. 114–15.

7. Ibid., p. 90.

8. Y. Congar, "My Pathfindings . . . ," p. 180.

9. O. Semmelroth, "The Priestly People of God and Its Official Ministers," *Concilium* 31 (Glen Rock, N.J.: Paulist Press, 1967), 100.

10. R. Vekemans, *Caesar and God* (Maryknoll: Orbis, 1972), p. 100.

11. K. Barth, *The Word of God and the Word of Man* (New York: Harper Torchbooks, 1957), p. 113.

12. Ibid., p. 114.

13. Ibid., p. 124.

14. Ibid., pp. 125–26.

15. R. Bultmann, *Jesus Christ and Mythology*, pp. 84–85.

16. K. Rahner, "What Is the Theological Starting Point for a Definition of the Priestly Ministry?," *Concilium* 43 (Paramus, N.J.: Paulist Press, 1969), p. 85.

17. J. Ratzinger, *Priestly Ministry: A Search for Its Meaning* (New York: Sentinel Press, 1971), p. 20 (reprinted from *Emmanuel*, Vol. 26, 1970).

18. *Lumen gentium*, Art. 28.

19. Quoted in Gustavo Gutierrez, *A Theology of Liberation* (Maryknoll: Orbis, 1973), p. 122, note 18.

20. P. J. Henriot, "Politics and the Priest," *Commonweal* 96 (1972), 498.

21. Synod document, "The Ministerial Priesthood," *Catholic Mind* 70 (1972), 45.

22. R. Vekemans, op. cit., pp. 95–118.

## CHAPTER XI

1. R. Bultmann, "New Testament and Mythology," in H. W. Bartsch (ed.), *Kerygma and Myth*, Vol. 1, p. 5.
2. Council of Trent, Fourth Session (1546), NR, 80; DS, 1501.
3. NR, 90; DS, 3011.
4. NR, 68; DS, 3541. Italics in original.
5. E. Mersch, *The Theology of the Mystical Body* (St. Louis: Herder, 1951), p. 413.
6. M.-D. Chenu, *La foi dans l'intelligence* (Paris: Cerf, 1964), p. 250; reprinted from his 1937 book, *La théologie au Saulchoir*.
7. *Dei verbum*, Art. 2.
8. G. Moran, *Theology of Revelation* (New York: Herder & Herder, 1966), p. 75.
9. G. Baum, *New Horizon*, p. 138.
10. K. Rahner, "Revelation," *Sacramentum Mundi* 5 (New York: Herder & Herder, 1969), p. 349.
11. The reasons for this statement are more fully developed in Chapter V above.
12. *Dei verbum*, Art. 4. The word "perfected" in the Abbott-Gallagher translation, which we are here following, is a mistranslation. It should read "perfects" (Latin, *perficit*).
13. Rom. 10:14–17.
14. For a sampling of these criticisms, see H. W. Bartsch (ed.), *Kerygma and Myth*, 2 vols. (London: SPCK, 1953, 1962).
15. *Dei verbum*, Art. 21.
16. *Gaudium et spes*, Art. 36.
17. Ibid., Art. 45. See also Arts. 10 and 22.
18. Ibid., Art. 44; cf. Art. 4.
19. Ibid., Art. 42.

## CHAPTER XII

1. B. J. F. Lonergan, *Method in Theology*, Chap. 10.
2. I am here advocating a collective and ecumenical application of the "presupposition" set forth by St. Ignatius of Loyola at the beginning of his *Spiritual Exercises*: "Let it be presupposed that every good Christian is more ready to save his neighbor's proposition than to condemn it."
3. H. R. Niebuhr, *Christ and Culture* (New York: Harper Torchbooks, 1951), pp. 238–39.
4. This term, popularized by Peter Berger in sociology, has ecclesiological implications, some of which are suggested by James A. Ecks in his article, "The Changing Church: Contributions from

Sociology," *American Benedictine Review* 23 (1972), 385–96.

5. The paragraphs that follow were already written before the author came across Rahner's very similar projections for tomorrow's Church. Rahner lists the following five characteristics: an open Church, an ecumenical Church, a Church built up out of voluntary base communities, a democratized Church, and a Church that is critical of the sociopolitical order. See K. Rahner, *Strukturwandel der Kirche als Aufgabe und Chance* (Freiburg: Herder, 1972), pp. 99–141.

6. *Gaudium et spes*, Art. 76.

7. On this and several other hypotheses for the future of the Church, see René Laurentin, *Réorientation de l'Eglise après le troisième synode* (Paris: Scuil, 1972), "Où va l'Eglise?" pp. 281–311.

8. Various "images for frontier life" are proposed by R. M. Brown in chapters 7 and 8 of his *Frontiers for the Church Today* (New York: Oxford University Press, 1973).

# Index

# OTHER IMAGE BOOKS

B 78 – 1